LIFE IN FREEDOM

BOOKS BY J. KRISHNAMURTI

THE IMMORTAL FRIEND (POEMS)
BY WHAT AUTHORITY
AT THE FEET OF THE MASTER
THE PATH
TEMPLE TALKS
THE SEARCH (POEMS)

J. KRISHNAMURTI
LIFE
IN FREEDOM

THE STAR PUBLISHING TRUST
HOLLAND

*This book has been compiled
by the Author from the Camp-
Fire addresses given in
Benares, Ojai and Ommen,
during 1928*

C O N T E N T S

informed persons had ascertained in 1811, as existing
between the eastern and western parts of the island,
and the country and towns. · The slaves have
increased largely in the eastern districts, but the
fearful certainty that, notwithstanding the importation of 185,000 new negroes, the mass of free colored
and slaves, mulattoes and blacks, had increased only
64,000, or one-fifth, between 1811 and 1825, exhibits
clearly that the changes experienced by the relations
of partial distribution, are reduced to much narrower
limits than might have been supposed.

Supposing the population, as already stated, to be
715,000 (which I believe to be within the minimum
number), the ratio of population in Cuba, in 1825,
is 197 individuals to the square league, and, consequently, nearly twice less than that of St. Domingo,
and four times smaller than that of Jamaica. If
Cuba were as well cultivated as the latter island, or,
more properly speaking, if the density of population
were the same, it would contain 3515 × 874 or
3,159,000 inhabitants;[1] that is to say, more than are

---

[1] Supposing the population of Haiti to be 820,000, it is 334 persons
to the square league, and if we estimate it at 936,000, it is 382.
Native writers suppose the island of Cuba to be capable of maintain-
ing seven and two-sevenths millions of inhabitants. (See Remon-
~~e of the Cuban Deputies, against the tariff of 1821, p. 9.)

now contained in the Republic of Colombia, or in all the archipelago of the Antilles. Yet Jamaica has 1,914,000 acres of waste land.

The most remote official census and statistics that I could obtain, during my residence in Havana, are those of 1774 and 1775, compiled by order of the Marquis de la Torre, and that of 1791, by order of Don Luis de las Casas.' Everyone is aware that both these were made with great negligence, and a large part of the population was omitted. The census of 1775, which is known as that of the Abbé Raynal, gives the following figures:

Even under this hypothesis, the ratio of population would not be equal to that of Ireland.—H.

' This governor was the founder of the Patriotic Society, the Board of Agriculture and Trade, the Chamber of Commerce, the Orphan Asylum, the Chair of Mathematics, and several primary schools. He intended to ameliorate the barbarous forms of criminal law, and created the noble office of advocate for the poor. The improvement and ornament of the city of Havana, the building of the highway to Guanajay, the construction of docks, the protection afforded to writers for the press, that they might give vigor to public spirit, all date from his time. Don Luis de las Casas y Aragorri, captain-general of Cuba (1790-1796), was born in the village of Sopuerta, in Biscay ; he fought with great distinction in Portugal, at Pensacola, in the Crimea, before Algiers, at Mahon, and at Gibraltar. He died in July, 1800, at Puerto Santa Maria, at the age of 65 years. See the compendiums of his life by friar ⬛⬛u Gonzalez, and by Don Tomas Romay.—H.

	Males.	Females.
Whites,	54,555	40,864
Free colored,	15,980	14,635
Slaves,	28,774	15,562
Total,	99,309	71,061

In all, 170,370, of which the district of Havana alone contained 75,607. I cannot answer for the correctness of this table, for I have not seen the official documents.

The census of 1791 gave 272,141 inhabitants, of which 137,800 were in the district of Havana, as follows: 44,337 in the capital, 27,715 in the other towns and villages of the district, and 65,748 in the country Partidos. These figures have been compared with the registers. A moment's reflection will demonstrate the contradictory nature of these results. The mass of 137,800 inhabitants in the district of Havana, are stated as follows; whites, 73,000, free colored, 27,600, slaves, 37,200; so that the whites would bear a proportion to the slaves of 2 to 1, instead of that of 100 to 83, which has long since been found to be the relative proportions, both in the city and in the country.

In 1804 I discussed the census of Don Luis de las Casas, with persons who possessed great knowledge of the locality. Examining the proportions of the numbers omitted in the partial comparisons, it seemed to us that the population of the island, in

1791, could not have been less than 362,700 souls. This has been augmented, during the years between 1791 and 1804, by the number of African negroes imported, which, according to the custom-house returns for that period, amounted to 60,393; by the immigration from Europe and St. Domingo (5,000); and by the excess of births and deaths, which, in truth, is indeed small in a country where one-fourth or one-fifth of the entire population is condemned to live in celibacy. The result of these three causes of increase, was estimated at 60,000, estimating an annual loss of seven per cent. on the newly imported negroes; this gives approximately, for the year 1804, a minimum of 432,080 inhabitants.[1]

[1] I estimated this number for the year 1804, to comprise, whites, 234,000, free-colored, 90,000, slaves, 180,000. (The census of 1817 has given, whites, 290,000, free colored, 115,000, and slaves, 225,000). I estimated the slave population, graduating the production of sugar at from 80 to 100 arrobes for each negro on the sugar plantations, and 82 slaves as the mean population of each plantation. There were, then, 250 of these. In the seven parishes, Guanajay, Managua, Batabanó, Güines, Cano, Bejucal, and Guanabacoa, there were found, by au exact census, 15,130 slaves on 183 sugar plantations.—(MSS. Documents, p. 134. *Representation of the Consulado of Havana*, 10th *July*, 1799.) It is difficult to ascertain correctly, the ratio of the production of sugar to the number of negroes employed on the estates, for there are some where barely 300 negroes produces 30,000 arrobes, while on others, 800 negroes produce only 27,000 arrobes yearly. The number of whites can be

The census of 1817 gives a population of 572,363, and this should be considered only as a minimum, corresponding with the results obtained by me, in 1804, and which have since been cited in many statistical works. The returns of the custom-houses alone show that more than 78,500 negroes were imported between 1804 and 1816.

The most valuable documents which we possess up to the present time (1825), relative to the population of the island, were published on the occasion of a celebrated motion made in the Spanish Cortes, on the 26th March 1811, by Señores Alcocer and Arguelles, against the African slave-trade in

estimated by the rolls of the militia, of which, in 1804, there were 2,680 disciplined, and 27,000 rural, notwithstanding the great facilities for avoiding the service, and the innumerable exemptions granted to lawyers, physicians, apothecaries, notaries, clergy and church servants, schoolmasters, overseers, traders, and all who are styled noble. See *Reflections of an Habanero upon the Independence of the Island*, 1823, *p.* 17. The number of men capable of bearing arms, between the ages of 15 and 60, was estimated, in 1817, as follows: 1st free class; whites, 71,047, mulattoes, 17,862, blacks, 17,246, total, 106,155; 2d slaves, 85,899, in all, 192,054. Taking as a basis, the estimate of the military enrolment of the population of France, (*Peuchet stat.* p. 243 *and* 247), we find that the number of 192,054 corresponds to a population somewhat less than six hundred thousand. The quota of the three classes, whites, free colored, and slaves, are as 37 : 18 : 45; while the relative proportions of the population are very nearly 46 : 18 : 36.—H.

general and the perpetual continuance of slavery in
the colonies. These valuable documents are accompanied and sustained by the remonstrance[1] which
Don Francisco de Arango (one of the wisest of
statesmen, and profoundly versed in everything
relating to his country), made to the Cortes, in the
the name of the Ayuntamiento, the Consulado, and
the Patriotic Society of Havana. It is there stated
that "there is no other general census than that
which was taken (in 1791), during the wise administration of Don Luis de las Casas, and that since that
time, some partial ones only have been taken in one
or other of the most populous districts."

From this we learn, that the tables published in
1811, are founded on incomplete data, and on
approximate estimates of the increase from 1791 to
that time. In the following table the division of the
island into four districts, has been adopted, as follows:—1st. The jurisdiction of Havana, or western part, between Cape San Antonio and Alvarez.
2d. The jurisdiction of Cuatro Villas, with its eight

---

[1] Representation of 16th August, 1811, which was made by the
Alferez Mayor of Havana, under direction of the Ayuntamiento,
Consulado, and Patriotic Society of that city, and laid before the
Cortes by these corporations. This representation, or remonstrance,
is contained in the *Documents relative to the slave-trade*, 1814, p.
1–86.—H.

districts. 3d. The jurisdiction of Puerto Principe, with seven districts. 4th. The jurisdiction of St. Jago de Cuba, with fifteen districts. The last three comprise the eastern part of the island.

	Whites.	Free colored.	Slaves.	Total.
WESTERN PART:				
Havana and Suburbs	43,000	27,000	28,000	98,000
Country...............	118,000	15,000	119,000	252,000
	161,000	42,000	147,000	350,000
EASTERN PART:				
St. Jago de Cuba........	40,000	38,000	32,000	110,000
Puerto Principe.........	38,000	14,000	18,000	70,000
Cuatro Villas	35,000	20,000	15,000	70,000
	113,000	72,000	65,000	250,000
Totals	274,000	114,000	212,000	600,000

The peaceful relations of the several castes with each other, will always be a political problem of the greatest importance, until such time as a wise legislation shall succeed in calming their inveterate hatred, by conceding an equality of civil rights to the oppressed classes. In 1811, the number of whites in the island of Cuba exceeded that of the slaves by 62,000, and was only one-fifth less than the aggregate of free colored and slaves. The whites in the English and French Antilles are nine per cent.,
Cuba they are forty-five per cent. of the

total population. The free colored amount to nineteen per cent., which is double their proportion in
Jamaica or Martinique. As the census of 1817,
modified by the Provincial Deputation, only exhibits
115,700 free colored, and 225,000 slaves, the comparison proves—1st, that the free colored have been
estimated incorrectly both in 1811 and 1817; and
2d, that the mortality of the negroes is so great that,
notwithstanding the importation of more than 67,700
negroes from Africa, according to the custom-house
returns, there were in 1817 only 13,300 more slaves
than in 1811.

The decrees of the Cortes of 3d March, and 26th
July, 1813, and the necessity of ascertaining the
population, for the establishment of the electoral
juntas of the province, the partido, and the parish,
obliged the government to take a new census in
1817, which is as follow:

*Census of 1817, exclusive of transient persons and
negroes imported during the year.*

Districts.	Whites.	Free colored.	Slaves.
Western Department:			
Havana	135,177	40,419	112,122
Matanzas	10,617	1,676	9,594
Trinidad (with Santi Espiritu,			
Remedios, and Villa Clara)	51,864	16,411	14,497

Districts.	Whites.	Free colored.	Slaves.
Eastern Department :			
Cuba (with Bayamo, Holguin, and Baracoa)	33,733	50,230	46,500
Puerto Principe	25,989	6,955	16,579
Total	257,380	115,691	199,292
In all	572,363.		

Though it may seem strange that the approximate estimate presented to the Cortes in 1811, shows a total population 28,000 greater than the actual census of 1817, this contradiction is only apparent. This census is doubtless less imperfect than that of 1791, yet it does not comprise all the population, because of the fear everywhere inspired in the people, by an operation which is always supposed by them to be not only direful, but the precursor of new taxation. On the other hand, the Provincial Deputation thought proper to make two modifications in the census of 1817, when sending it to Madrid : 1st, adding 32,641 whites (transient traders and crews of vessels), whose business call them to Cuba; and 2d, adding 25,967 African negroes imported during the year 1817. By these additions the Provincial Deputation obtained a total population of 630,980, of which 290,021 were whites, 115,691 free colored, and 225,261 slaves.[1]

[1] So far as my opinion goes, I believe that in 1825 there were

We shall not be surprised at the partial contradictions found in the tables of population in America, when we take into consideration all the difficulties that have been encountered in the centres of European civilization, England and France, whenever the great operation of a general census is attempted. No one is ignorant, for example, of the fact, that the population of Paris, in 1820, was 714,000, and from the number of deaths, and supposed proportion of births to the total population, it is believed to have been 520,000, at the beginning of the eighteenth century; yet, during the administration of Mon. Neckar, the ascertained population was one-sixth less than this number. It is known, that, from 1801 to 1821, the population of England and Wales increased 3,104,683, yet the registers of births and deaths show an increase of only 2,173,416; and it is impossible to attribute the difference of 931,267 to immigration from Ireland. These examples do not ·prove that we should distrust the calculations of

nearly 325,000 whites, and one the best informed gentlemen of Havana, who was well acquainted with the country, estimated them, in 1823, at 340,000. (See *On Independence of Cuba*, p. 17.) In some parts of the island statistical tables have been formed with great care; in San Juan de los Remedios, and Filipinas, for example, particularly those made by Don Joaquin Vigil y Quiñones and Don José Aguilar, in 1819.—H.

political economy; what they do prove is, that we should not employ numerical elements, without having first examined them, and ascertained the extent of their errors. One is tempted to compare the different degrees of probability presented· by statistical tables in the Ottoman Empire, in Spanish and Portuguese America, in France or Prussia, by geographical positions based on the eclipses of the moon, on its distance from the sun, or on occultations of the stars.

In order to adapt a census made twenty years since, to any other given time, we must ascertain the rate of increase; but this can be ascertained only from the enumerations of 1791, 1810, and 1817, taken in the eastern part of the island, which is the least populous portion. When comparisons rest upon too small masses, existing under the influence of particular circumstances (as, in seaports or in the sugar planting districts), they cannot give the numerical results proper to be used as a basis for the entire country.

·It is generally supposed that the whites increase more rapidly in the villages and haciendas than in the towns; that the free colored, who prefer a make-shift residence in the towns to the labors of agriculture, multiply with greater rapidity than all the other classes; and that the slaves, among whom, unfortunately, there are only one-third of the females required by the number of males,[1] decrease more than eight per cent., annually.

We have already seen[2] that in Havana and suburbs, the whites increased 78 per cent., and the free colored 171 per cent., in twenty years. Through nearly all the eastern part of the island, the same classes have nearly doubled in the same time. We will here mention that the free colored multiply, in part, through the transition from one class to the other, and the slaves increase through the activity of the slave-trade. At the present time, the whites receive but little increase through immigration from Europe, the Canary Islands, the Antilles, or the Continent; this class multiplies within itself, for *patents of white blood* are seldom granted by the tribunals to persons of light yellow color.

According to the census of 1775, the district of Havana, comprising six cities (the capital, Trinidad, San Felipe y Santiago, Santa Maria del Rosario, Jaruco, and Matanzas), six towns (Guanabacoa, Santi Espiritu, Villa Clara, San Antonio, San Juan de los Remedios, and Santiago), and thirty villages and hamlets, contained a population of 171,626; and in

---

[1] This applies only to those slaves employed on the sugar plantations.

[2] Chapter I., p. 114.

1806, with greater exactitude, 277,364. (*Patriota Americano*, vol. ii., p. 300.) Consequently, the increase, in thirty-one years, had been only sixty-one per cent.; but if we could compare the latter half of this term, it would show a much more rapid increase. In fact, the census of 1817 gives a population of 392,377, which shows an increase of forty-one per cent., in eleven years, for the same extent of country, then called the Province of Havana, comprising the districts of the capital, Matanzas, and Trinidad, or Cuatro Villas.

We must remember, while comparing the results of the censuses of 1791 and 1810 of the capital and of the eastern province, that we obtain an excessive rate of increase, for there were many more omissions in the first than in the second census. By comparing those most recently taken in the eastern province, in 1810 and 1817, I believe we approach nearer the truth. These are as follows:

	Whites.	Free Col'd.	Slaves.	Total.
1810	35,513	32,884	38,834	107,231
1817	33,733	50,230	46,500	130,463

Increase in six years 23,232, or more than twenty-one per cent.; and there is probably an error in the second statement of the number of whites, in the last census. The proportion of whites and free colored is very great in the district of Cuatro Villas,

where, in the six partidos of San Juan de los Remedios, San Augustin, San Anastasio de Cupey, San
Felipe, Santa Fé, and Sagua la Chica, there were, in
1819, in an area of 24,651 *caballerias*, a total population of 13,722, of which 9,572 were whites, 2,000
free colored, and 2,140 slaves; while, on the contrary, in the ten partidos of the Filipinas district, in
the same year, in a population of 13,026, there were
5,871 whites, 3,521 free colored, and 3,634 slaves.
The proportion of free colored to white was as 1 to 1.7.

[NOTE.—Since the publication of the foregoing
admirable analysis by Baron Humboldt, of the population of Cuba, censuses have been taken in the
years 1827, 1841, and 1846, which are as follows:

CENSUS OF 1827.

Department.	Whites.		Free Colored.		Slaves.		Total.
	Male.	Female.	Male.	Female.	Male.	Female.	
Western,..	89,526	75,582	21,235	24,829	125,883	72,027	408,587
Central,...	58,447	44,776	13,296	10,950	28,398	13,680	164,497
Eastern, ..	25,680	22,090	17,431	18,758	29,504	17,995	131,458
Total,...	168,658	142,898	51,962	54,532	183,290	103,652	704,486

CENSUS OF 1841.

	Male.	Female.	Male.	Female.	Male.	Female.	Total.
Western,..	135,079	108,944	32,726	38,787	207,954	118,320	681,760
Central,...	60,085	53,888	15,525	16,054	84,989	15,217	195,608
Eastern, ..	32,080	28,365	27,452	27,344	88,357	26,708	130,256
Total,...	227,144	191,147	75,708	77,185	281,250	155,245	1,007,624

CENSUS OF 1846.

Department.	Whites.		Free Colored.		Slaves.		Total.
	Male.	Female.	Male.	Female.	Male.	Female.	
Western,..	189,968	110,141	28,964	32,730	140,131	87,683	588,616
Central,...	62,262	52,692	17,041	17,074	32,425	14,560	196,054
Eastern, ..	84,758	81,951	26,646	26,771	28,455	20,506	169,082
Total....	280,968	194,784	72,651	76,575	201,011	122,748	898,752

The slightest examination leads to the belief that there is some error in the figures of the census of 1846; and we are inclined to doubt its results, for the following reasons:

1st. During the period between 1841 and 1846, no great cause, as epidemic, or emigration on a large scale, existed to check the hitherto steady increase of the slave population, and cause a decrease of 112,736 in its numbers, being nearly twenty six per cent. of the returns of 1841; which apparent decrease, and the annihilation of former rate of increase (3.7 per cent., yearly), amount together to a loss of 47 per cent., in six years.

2d. During this period, the material prosperity of the country experienced no decrease, except the loss of part of one crop, consequent upon the hurricane of 1845.

3d. During the period from 1842 to 1846, the church returns of christenings and interments were as follows:

	Whites.	Colored.	Total.
Christenings,..	87,047	74,302	161,349
Interments,...	51,456	57,762	109,218
Increase, ...	35,591	16,540	52,131

4th. And because, that, in addition to the reasons adduced by Baron Humboldt, for less returns by the people than their actual numbers, that the taking of a census "is always supposed by them to be not only direful, but the precursor of new taxation;" a capitation tax upon house servants was imposed in 1844, and a very general fear existed that it would be extended to other classes.

When the writer first went to Cuba, in 1834, he was strongly impressed with the popular supposition there, that the slave population diminished fully eight per cent. annually, by death, and that this loss was only partially compensated (about three per cent.), by the importation of negroes from Africa, which, at that time was not supposed to reach twelve thousand a year. At this period, the mean annual export of sugar was 550,000 boxes, and of coffee, 330,000 bags (the two great staples), and the mean annual value of imports was $17,000,000, and of exports, $14,000,000, according to the official valuations. During the seventeen years of our residence there, the annual export of sugar steadily increased until it exceeded 1,500,000 boxes; that of

coffee fell to 125,000 bags, and the value of imports
and exports reached $29,750,000 and $27,450,000 respectively.

Admitting as correct the supposed annual loss
of five per cent. to the slave or laboring population, the producing class must have diminished
eighty-five per cent. from 1835 to 1852, a supposition directly at variance with the results exhibited
by the commerce of the island. So far as our
limited individual observation extended, we arrived
at the conclusion that this supposition of loss arose
from the fact that the greater part of capital and
scientific knowledge in Cuba is absorbed in the
sugar culture, and that the estimates regarding
population were based, in a great measure, on data
derived from this class and branch of labor. Its
great preponderance in the foreign commerce of the
island, overshadowed its true relation to the general
economy of the country. We believe that the slave
population of Cuba does not decrease in the towns,
nor on the coffee estates, tobacco plantations, grazing
farms, and numerous minor branches of agriculture,
but that on the contrary, it increases in all these,
and more than compensates for the loss on the sugar
plantations. The supposed former rate of loss has
been greatly diminished during the last twenty
years, by the improvements in the system of con-

ducting the sugar plantations, and a greater equalization of sexes upon them. In no other way can we account for the rapid increase in the material prosperity of Cuba, an increase that is only surpassed by that of our own United States.

In estimating, therefore, the present population of Cuba, we shall adopt the rate of increase exhibited by the two censuses of 1827 and 1841. The first may be considered the minimum of population at that time, it being less than the well-reasoned estimate of Baron Humboldt for the year 1825: and although the second was perhaps taken with greater care, we know of no reason why it should not be held also as the minimum expression of the population. It was, at the time of publication, charged by well-informed writers, with understating numbers.

The annual rate per cent. of increase in the several classes of population, as indicated by the various censuses, is somewhat fluctuating, and is as follows:

	White.	Free colored.	Slaves.
1774 to 1792,	2.7	4.2	5
1792 " 1817,	3.1	4.4	5.4
1817 " 1827,	2.1	0.68	4.4
1827 " 1841,	2.5	8.1	3.7

The latter rate of increase would give to Cuba, at the close of the year 1855,

Whites,... ..564,693, being 39 per cent.
Free colored,.219,170,   "   15 "   "
Slaves,......662,599,   "   46 "   "
              _____
       Total,....1,446,462

This does not seem excessive, when we take into consideration her vast consumption of foreign products, and the great value of the staples she pours into the lap of commerce.]

CHAPTER VI.

SLAVERY.

Manumission frequent in Cuba—Its causes—Slaves allowed to hire their time. [NOTE—Usual wages—Number of working days—Slaves may purchase their freedom by partial payments—Many remain partially redeemed — Reason — Curious phase of negro mind.] Position of free negroes—Mild laws—Slaves previous to the Eighteenth century—Religious scruples regarding females—Population of Sugar plantations—Projects for increasing slaves—Don Francisco de Arango—Desire to ameliorate their condition—First importation—Entire importation to America in sixteenth century—Slaves in Cuba in 1763—Activity of trade at the close of the eighteenth century—Treaty with England. [NOTE—Total number imported.] Compared with Jamaica — Other English colonies (*note*)—Humane result in Cuba—Mortality of slaves—Has diminished—Of newly imported negroes—Means to prevent decrease—Abolition of slave-trade. [NOTE—Not effective—Baron Humboldt's sketch of slavery in Cuba—Decrease of slaves a fallacy—Increase only paralleled in United States—Their well-being evident—Chinese imported—Injurious influence and evil results.

IN no part of the world, where slavery exists, is manumission so frequent as in the island of Cuba; for Spanish legislation, directly the reverse of French and English, favors in an extraordinary degree the

attainment of freedom, placing no obstacle in its
way, nor making it in any manner onerous. The
right which every slave has of seeking a new master, or purchasing his liberty, if he can pay the
amount of his cost; the religious sentiment that in-
duces many persons in good circumstances to con-
cede by will freedom to a certain number of negroes;
the custom of retaining a number of both sexes for
domestic service, and the affections that necessarily
arise from this familiar intercourse with the whites;
and the facilities allowed to slave-workmen to labor
for their own account, by paying a certain stipulated
sum to their masters, are the principal causes why
so many blacks acquire their freedom in the towns.[1]

[1] The customary rate of hire is ten cents on each $100 of
the value of the slave for every working-day. There are about
two hundred and ninety working-days in the year, Sundays and
church holidays being considered days of rest. In addition to the
above-mentioned facilities for attaining freedom, the slave has the
privilege of paying his master small sums of money on account, and
thus becoming a coöwner of himself. Thus, if his value be $600,
by paying his master $25 he becomes the owner of one twenty-
fourth of himself; when he has paid $50, he owns one-twelfth, and
so on; and in hiring his time, he pays to his master rent only on the
sum remaining due. The law obliges the master to accept these
partial payments; and should the owner over-value the slave at the
time of commencing them, the negro can appeal to the syndic, who
is annually appointed to protect the slaves. A slave who has partially manumitted himself is styled *coartado*. Many redeem them-

The position of the free negroes in Cuba is much better than it is elsewhere, even among those nations which have for ages flattered themselves as being most advanced in civilization. We find there no such barbarous laws as have been invoked, even in our own days, by which free negroes are prohibited from receiving donations from the whites, and can be deprived of their liberty, and sold for the benefit of the State, should they be convicted of affording an asylum to escaped slaves.[1]

Until the closing years of the eighteenth century, the number of slaves on the sugar plantations in Cuba was extremely small, and what most surprises us is, that a prejudice founded on " religious scruples," opposed the introduction there of females (they costing in Havana one-third less than males), thus forcing

selves excepting the sum of $50 or $100; and on this pay a rent to the master for the rest of their lives, no matter how much wealth they may acquire. A careful study of individual reasons, among the blacks in Cuba, for adopting this course, might perhaps develop some unobserved peculiarities of the negro mind. It may sometimes arise from ties of affection, sometimes from interests, and it may be found to result, in some cases, from an intuitive desire, or an idiosyncrasy on the part of the negro to have some immediate and tangible superior, to whose opinion he can look with respect, and from whom he can claim protection in calamity.

[1] Decision of the Supreme Council of Martinique of 4th July, 1720.—" Decree of 1st March, 1766, § 7.—H.

the slaves to celibacy, under the pretext that vicious habits were thus avoided. The Jesuits and the Bethlemite friars, being superior to this sad prejudice, were the only planters that allowed them on their plantations. Although the census of 1775, which is undoubtedly very imperfect, gave 15,562 female and 29,336 male slaves, we must bear in mind that this census embraced the whole island, while the sugar plantations, even at the present time (1825), do not contain more than one-fourth of the entire slave population.[1]

From the year 1795, the Consulado of Havana

---

[1] The "Cuadro Estadistico." of 1846 presents some partial information on this point, which is interesting. It states the number of sugar plantations in the several departments of the island and their population, as follows :—

	Plantations.	Population.	Average.
Western	785	96,462	131
Central	404	23,763	59
Eastern	303	10,586	35
	1442	130,816	

These numbers are undoubtedly under-stated ; but estimating an average of ten per cent. as the white population of the sugar plantations, we have a slave population of 116,735, being nearly 18 per cent., engaged in the culture of sugar. It is to be regretted that the "Cuadro" does not state the relative numbers of males and females; but well-informed persons think the sugar plantations have now one-third females.

have seriously entertained projects for increasing the slave population, independent of the fluctuations of the slave-trade. Don Francisco de Arango, whose labors have always been pure and judicious, proposed the imposition of a tax upon those plantations which did not contain one-third females among their slaves. He also proposed the imposition of a duty of six dollars upon each male negro imported from Africa. Although these measures were not adopted, for the colonial juntas always refused to adopt coercive measures, yet, from that time, there has arisen a desire to increase the number of marriages, and to take better care of the children of the slaves; and a royal order (22 April, 1804) recommends this policy to "the sense of right, and the humanity of the colonists."

The census of 1817 gave, according to Poinsett, 60,822 female, and 106,521 male slaves. In 1771, the proportion of female to male slaves was 1 to 1.9; so that, in forty years, it had altered very slightly, it being, in 1817, 1 to 1.7. The small amount of this change must be attributed to the large number of African negroes imported subsequently to 1791, and to the fact that the importation of females has been large, only during the years between 1817 and 1820: the slaves retained as servants in the cities are only a small fraction of the total number. In the district of Batabanó, which contained in 1818 a population

of 2,078, with 13 sugar, and 7 coffee estates, there
were 2,226 male, and 257 female slaves; proportion,
8 to 1. In San Juan de los Remedios, containing, in
1817, a population of 13,700, with 17 sugar, and 78
coffee estates, there were 1,200 male and 660 female
slaves; proportion, 19 to 1.[1] In the district of Feli-
.pinas, having in 1819 a population of 13,026, there
were 2,494 male, and 997 female slaves; proportion,
2.4 to 1. In all the island, the males are to the
females as 1.7 to 1; on the sugar estates alone, they
are barely 4 to 1.

The first introduction of negroes (in the eastern
part of the island), occurred in 1521. At that time,
the Spaniards were much less desirous than the Portuguese of possessing slaves; for, in 1539, twelve
thousand negroes were sold in the city of Lisbon.
The trade in slaves was not free in the sixteenth century, licenses for it being granted by the government; and, in 1586, Gaspar Peralta purchased the
monopoly for the whole of Spanish America. In
1595, it was sold to Gomez Raynal; and again, in
1615, to Antonio Rodriguez de Elvas.

The entire American importation then did not
exceed 3,500, yearly; and the people of Cuba, occupied exclusively in raising cattle, received very few.
During the war of the succession, the French traders

---

[1] Thus in the original.

visited Havana, exchanging slaves for tobacco. The possession of the island by the English stimulated somewhat the importation of negroes; yet, in 1763, although the capture of Havana, and the presence of foreigners, created new wants, the number of slaves did not exceed 25,000 in that district, and 32,000 in the whole island.

The number of Africans imported from 1521 to 1763, was probably 60,000, whose descendants exist among the free mulattoes, the greater part of which inhabit the eastern part of the island. From 1763 to 1790, when the trade in negroes was thrown open, Havana received 24,875 (by the Tobacco Company 4,957 from 1763 to 1766; by the contract with the Marquis de Casa Enrile, 14,132, from 1773 to 1779; by the contract with Baker and Dawson, 5,786, from 1786 to 1789). If we estimate the importation of slaves in the eastern part of the island, during these twenty-seven years (1763 to 1790), at 6,000, we have a total importation of 90,875 from the time of the discovery of Cuba, or more properly speaking, from 1521 to 1790.

The activity of the slave-trade in the fifteen years following 1790, was so great, that more slaves were bought and sold in that time, than in the two and a half centuries that preceded its being thrown open. This activity was redoubled when England stipulated

with Spain, that the trade should be suppressed
north of the equator from the 22d November, 1817,
and totally abolished on the 30th May 1820. The
King of Spain accepted from England (a fact which
posterity will hardly believe), the sum of four hundred thousand pounds sterling, in compensation for
the damages and loss which might arise from the
cessation of this barbarous traffic.

The following statement exhibits the number of
African negroes imported in Havana alone, according
to the custom-house returns.

1790....2,534	1806....4,395
1791... 8,498	1807....2,565
1792....8,528	1808 ...1,607
1793....3,777	1809....1,162
1794....4,164	1810....6,672
1795....5,832	1811....6,349
1796....5,711	1812....6,081
1797....4,552	1813....4,770
1798....2,001	1814....4,321
1799 ...4,919	1815....9,111
1800....4,145	1816...17,737
1801....1,659	1817[1].. 25,841
1802...13,832	1818...19,902
1803....9,671	1819...17,194
1804....8,923	1820....4,122
1805....4,999	—— ——

Total, in 31 years,....225,574

[1] Other MS. notes in my possession state the number for 1817, at
23,560 slaves.—H.

The mean annual number during this interval is
7,470, and 11,542 for the last ten years. This should
be increased at least one-fourth, partly, because of
the illicit importations, and omissions in the returns,
and partly for the licit importations at Trinidad
and St. Jago; so that we have for the whole island,

                    From 1521 to 1763.....60,000
                     "   1764 " 1790.....33,409

In Havana alone,

                    From 1791 to 1805......91,211
                     "   1806 " 1820.....131,829
                                          ———————
                                          316,449

Increase by the illicit trade and
by the importations in the eastern
part of the island, from 1791 to 1820,.. ...56,000
                                          ———————
                                          372,449

[NOTE.—In order to present in one continuous
view the number of negroes carried to Cuba up to
the latest returns accessible to us, we continue here
the calculation by Baron Humboldt. From the
reports of the British commissioners at Havana, we
learn the following particulars, in relation to the
trade subsequently to its suppression in 1820, by the
treaty with England.

In 1821, twenty-six vessels arrived, bringing 6,415
slaves; and Mr. Jameson, one of the commissioners,
states that to this amount one-half should be added
for importations not ascertained by the commis-

sioners, and that he estimates the slaves imported during that year at 10,000.

The yearly reports of the commissioners give the following figures, up to 1828 :

1822	10 vessels arrived—estimated,			3,000
1823	4	"	"	1,200
1824	17	"	"	5,100
1825	14	"	"	4,200
1826	11	"	"	*3,000
1827	10	"	"	*3,500
1828	28	"	"	*7,000
				27,000
Add Mr. Jameson's estimate of one-half,				13,500
Making a total of				40,500

A report of the British consul at Havana, to the foreign office in London, gives the following statement of slaves imported into Cuba from 1829 to 1838; to which, he estimates, one-fifth should be added for non-ascertained importations :

1829	8,600		1834	11,400
1830	9,800		1835	14,800
1831	10,400		1836	14,200
1832	8,200		1837	15,200
1833	9,000			
			Total,	101,600
			Add one-fifth,,	20,320
				121,920

* These numbers are given by the commissioners, in their reports; for the other years, the number of vessels arriving only is stated.

The importations from 1838 to 1853, according to the returns laid before the British House of Commons, were as follows:

1838	10,495	1846	419
1839	10,995	1847	1,450
1840	10,104	1848	1,500
1841	8,893	1849	8,700
1842	3,630	1850	3,500
1843	8,000	1851	5,000
1844	10,000	1852	7,924
1845	1,300	30 June, '53	7,329
			99,239

We may, therefore, estimate the total number of negroes imported into Cuba from the coast of Africa, as follows:

To 1820 according to Baron Humboldt,	372,449
1821 " " Mr. Jameson,	10,000
1822 to 1828	40,500
1829 to 1837	121,920
1838 to 30 June, 1853	99,239
	644,108] [1]

[1] While these pages were going through the press, we received from the British Foreign Office, through the kind attention of Hon. John Appleton, secretary to the legation of the United States at London, a copy of a parliamentary return to the British House of Commons, ordered to be printed on the 11th of April 1845, according to which, the importations of slaves in Spanish territory in

We have seen that Jamaica has received from Africa,[1] during these three centuries, 850,000 negroes; and, according to a more exact statement, nearly 677,000 in the one hundred and eight years, from 1700 to 1808, and yet that island contains now but 380,000 blacks and mulattoes, free and slave. The island of Cuba presents a more humane result,

America (Cuba and Porto Rico, the number for the latter being very small), from 1821 to 1843 inclusive, amounted to 75,653

  If to this number we add importations to 1820, according to Baron Humboldt, ... 372,449

  1844 to June 30, 1853, as above, ... 47,122

We have a total of 495,224

This number is largely exceeded by the estimate we have given above. The several parliamentary returns before us do not agree with each other, nor with the reports of the British commissioners at Havana. With the exception of those for the term from 1832 to 1837, our figures have been obtained from the annual reports of the Havana commissioners to the British government, and represent the maximum of slave importations in Cuba. Through the same polite attentions, we learn that the number of slaves illegally imported into Cuba, during the years 1853 and 1854, has been 12,500, and 10,230, respectively.

[1] All the English colonies in the Antilles, which at the present time contain only about 700,000 blacks and mulattoes, free and slave, have received, in one hundred and six years, from 1680 to 1786 - - - .own by the custom-house returns, 2,130,000 negroes of Africa.—H.

for it contains 130,000 free colored, while Jamaica has only 35,000, with a population of one-half greater. Cuba has received from Africa,

Previous to 1791	93,500
From 1791 to 1825, at least	320,000
	413,500

In 1825, in consequence of the small number of females brought by the traders, there existed in the island only,

Negroes, free and slave	320,000
Mulattoes	70,000
	390,000

A similar calculation was sent to the Cortes of Spain, on the 20 July 1811, based upon numerical elements differing slightly from these, in which it was endeavored to prove that the island of Cuba had received up to 1810, less than 229,000 African negroes,[1] which are represented, in 1811, by a slave

---

[1] According to a note published by the Consulado of Havana (Papal Periodico. 1801, p. 12), it is estimated that the average cost of the 15,647 African negroes, imported from 1797 to 1800, was $375, each. At this rate, the 307,000 imported from 1790 to 1823, will have cost the inhabitants of the island the sum of $115,125,000.—H.

and free population of blacks and mulattoes, amounting to 326,000; being an excess of 97,000 over the number imported.[1] When it is remembered that the whites have contributed to the existence of 70,000 mulattoes,[2] leaving aside the natural increase that has resulted from so many thousand negroes progressively imported, one exclaims, "What other nation, or human society, can give so favorable an

[1] My calculation closes with 1825, and the number of negroes imported since the *conquest* amounts to 413,500. The calculation sent to the Cortes closes with 1810, and gives 229,000. (*Documentos*, p. 119.) Difference, 184,500; but, according to the returns of the Havana custom-house alone, the number of African negroes brought to that port from 1811 to 1820, has been 109,000, and to this we must add, 1st, according to the principles admitted by the consulado, one-fourth or 27,000, for the licit importations at other ports of the island; and, 2d, the amount of illicit traffic, from 1811 to 1825.—H.

[2] The work undertaken by the consulado, in 1811, relative to the probable distribution of 326,000 blacks, free and slave, contains some very interesting matter, which great local knowledge alone could have supplied to that body. A. *Cities*. Western part.—In Havana, 27,000 free colored, and 28,000 slaves; seven towns, with Ayuntamiento, 18,000; from which we have, in the jurisdiction of Havana, 36,000 free colored, and 37,000 slaves. Eastern part, 86,000 free colored, and 32,000 slaves. Total, in the cities, 72,000 free colored, and 69,000 slaves, or 141,000. B. *Country*.—Jurisdiction of Havana, 6,000 free colored, and 110,000 slaves. Eastern part, 36,000 free colored, and 33,000 slaves. Total, in the country, 185,000.—*Documentos sobre los negros*, p. 121.—H.

account of the results of this *unfortunate trade !*"
I respect the sentiments that have dictated these
lines, and will again repeat, that if we compare.
Cuba with Jamaica, the results appear in favor of
the Spanish legislation, and the customs of the inhabitants of Cuba. These comparisons demonstrate a
state of affairs in the latter island infinitely more
favorable to the physical preservation and manumission of the negroes; but what a sorrowful spectacle
is presented by Christian and civilized nations dis-
puting which of the two, in three centuries, has
destroyed the least number of Africans, by reducing
them to slavery !

I will not praise the treatment of the negroes in
the southern portion of the United States,[1] but
certain it is, that different degrees exist in the
sufferings of the human species. The slave who has
a cabin and a family, is not so unhappy as he who is
folded as if he were one of a flock of sheep. The
greater the number of slaves established_with their

---

[1] See "*Negro slavery in the United States of America and
Jamaica*," 1823, p. 31, as to the comparative state of misery
between the slaves of the Antilles, and those of the United States.
In 1823 Jamaica had 170,466 males, and 171,916 females; the
United States, in 1820, had 788,020 males, and 750,100 females. It
is not, therefore, the disproportion between the sexes that causes the
absence of natural increase in the Antilles.—H.

10*

families, in cabins which they deem their own, the more rapid is their multiplication. The slaves in the United States were as follows:—

1770....480,000	1810....1,191,364
1791... 676,696	1820....1,541,568
1800....894,444	

The annual increase[1] for the last ten years, has been (without counting the manumission of 100,000), 26,000, which is doubling in 27 years. I will say, therefore, with Mr. Cropper,[2] that if the slaves in Jamaica and Cuba had multiplied in the same proportion,[3] these two islands would have had, one

[1] The increase of the slaves from 1790 to 1810 (514,668), arises as follows:—1st. The natural increase in the families; 2d. The importation of 30,000 negroes, between 1804 and 1808, which was, unhappily, permitted by the Legislature of South Carolina; 3d. The acquisition of Louisiana, where there were 30,000 negroes. The increase from the last two causes has been only $\frac{1}{4}$ of the total increase, and has been compensated by the manumission of more than 100,000 negroes, who, in 1810, ceased to appear in the slave returns. The slaves multiply somewhat less rapidly (the exact proportion being 0.02611 to 0.02915), than the total population of the United States; but their multiplication is more rapid than that of the whites, wherever they form a considerable portion of the population, as in the southern states. (*Morse's Mod. Geogr.* 1822, p. 608.)—H.

[2] Letter addressed to the Liverpool Society, 1823, p. 18.—H.

[3] The number of 480,000, in the year 1770, is not based upon an actual census, it being only an approximate estimate. Albert

in 1795, and the other in 1800, very nearly their present population, without any necessity of loading 400,000 negroes with chains, in Africa, and dragging them to Port Royal or Havana.

The mortality of the negroes varies greatly in Cuba, according to the kind of labor, the humanity of the masters or overseers, and the number of women employed in taking care of the sick. I have

Gallatin thinks that the United States, which, at the close of 1823, had a population of 1,665,000 slaves, and 250,000 free colored, being a total of 1,915,000 blacks and mulattoes, never received from the coast of Africa over 300,000 negroes, that is to say, 1,183,000 less than those received from 1680 to 1786, by the English Antilles, the black and mulatto population of which, now barely exceeds one-third part of that of the United States.—H.

Mr. Carey, of Pennsylvania, in his work on the slave-trade, says, "the trade in negro slaves to the American colonies was too small to attract attention." After a close argument from the ratio of increase since the first census, Mr. C. is enabled to recur back, and compute the population at earlier periods, separating the native born from importations. Setting out with the fact that the slaves (blacks), numbered 55,850 in 1714, he finds that there were brought, of these,

From Africa,			30,000
Importation from 1715 to 1750			90,000
"	"	1751 " 1760	85,000
"	"	1761 " 1770	74,000
"	"	1771 " 1790	84,000
"	"	1790 " 1808	70,000
		Total number imported,	833,000

Compend. of Census of U. States, 1850, p. 83, note.

heard discussed with the greatest coolness, the question whether it was better for the proprietor not to overwork his slaves, and consequently have to replace them with less frequency, or whether he should get all he could out of them in a few years, and thus have to purchase newly imported Africans more frequently. But these are the reasonings of avarice when one man holds another in servitude.

It would be unjust to deny that the mortality of the blacks has diminished greatly in Cuba, within the last fifteen years. Many proprietors have studied how they might best improve the rules of their plantations. The mean mortality of the newly imported negroes is still from ten to twelve per cent.,[1] and from observations made on several well conducted sugar plantations, it may fall to even six or eight per cent. This loss among the newly imported negroes varies much according to the time of their arrival; the most favorable season for them is from October until January, those being the most healthy months, and most abundant in provisions on

[1] We are assured that in Martinique, where there are 78,000 slaves, the mean mortality is 6,000, while the births are barely 1,290, yearly. Before the cessation of the slave-trade, Jamaica lost annually, 7,000, or 2½ per cent.; since that time, the diminution of the population is scarcely perceptible.—*Review of the Registry Laws by the Com. of the Afric. Inst.* 1820, p. 43.—H.

the plantations. In the hot months, the mortality *during the sale* is sometimes four per cent., as was the case in 1802.

An increase in the number of female slaves, so useful in the care of their husbands and their sick companions; their relief from labor during pregnancy; greater attention to their children; the establishment of the slaves by families in separate cabins; an abundance of food; an increase in the number of days of rest; and the introduction of a system of moderate labor for their own account, are the most powerful and the only means to prevent the diminution in numbers of the blacks. Some persons who are well informed as to the old system on the plantations, believe that in the present state of things, the number of slaves would diminish five per cent. annually if the contraband traffic should entirely cease. This diminution is nearly equal to that of the English Lesser Antilles, except Santa Lucia and Granada. These last, forewarned by the discussions in Parliament, took measures to increase the importation of females. The abolition of the African slave-trade in Cuba has been more prompt and more unexpected

[Note.—The illustrious author's anticipations in regard to the cessation of the African slave-trade in

Cuba, have not been realized; it being matter of
public notoriety that it is still carried on there on a
large scale, with the connivance of the government,
and in flagrant opposition to the known wishes of
the great majority of the Cubans.   His sketch of
slavery, as it exists in that island, is worthy the
careful attention of men of every opinion regarding
the institution itself.   We have spoken elsewhere [1]
of what we deem the fallacy of the decrease of the
slaves in Cuba by death; but a conclusive argument on this point is presented in the fact that while,
by a liberal computation, there have been imported
into Cuba 644,108 Africans, there are now in that
island 662,599 slaves, and 219,170 free blacks,
making a total of 881,769 Africans and their descendants, while in all the English Antilles an
importation of 2,130,000 negroes was represented
by 700,000 in 1825.—(See note to p.192, chap. V.)
This result has only been paralleled in the Southern
States of our own confederacy, for even in the free
negro islands of the American Mediterranean, we
are led, by the best information we can obtain, to
suppose that the black population, as well as the
white, experiences a constant decrease.   If it be
true that population can increase only under a con-

[1] See note at the close of Chapter V.

dition of physical well-being, and that a decrease denotes a condition of physical suffering, the situation of the negro in Cuba must be vastly superior to that of his own race in the free islands. That his moral condition exhibits the same result we believe will be admitted by every impartial traveller in the two countries.

Another element has been introduced in the population of Cuba, by the importation of several thousands of Chinese, who are contracted to labor on the sugar estates for a period of years, at prices far below the usual value of labor in the island. The class of persons contracted with is usually the lowest of the low in the crowded sea-ports of China. No females are brought, and they are thus forced to amalgamate with the slave population, to whom they bring neither honest principles nor good morals. No one who for a moment contemplates the inevitable consequences of this resort of English philanthropy to remedy its social errors, can doubt its results; the amalgamation of unequal and dissonant races of men in their most degraded condition, can only be productive of the greatest moral and social evils to the community upon which it is forced.]

CHAPTER VII.

RACES.

But two now in the Antilles—Indians have disappeared—Confusion of early historians relative to their numbers—Character of estimates by early voyagers—Why Cuba might not have been as populous as represented—Cruelties of first settlers—Early mode of computing population—Movement of colonization in Cuba—Law of proportion of races—Havana—Cuatro Villas—Puerto Principe—St. Jago de Cuba—Density of population—Populous and uninhabited districts—Impossibility of the military defence of the island—Intellectual culture—Intelligence of the Habaneros—Apparent distance from Europe diminished—Declining influence of the old Spaniards—Admirable institutions in Havana—The necessity of reform.

As the primitive population of the Antilles has entirely disappeared (the Caribbean *zambos*, a mixture of natives and blacks, having been removed from the island of San Vicente to Ratan, in 1796) we must consider their present population (2,850,000), as being entirely of European and African blood. The pure blacks form nearly two-thirds of it, the whites one-sixth, and the mixed races one-seventh. In the Spanish colonies on the continent, we find the descendants of the Indians who have disappeared among the *mestizos* and *sambos* (crossings of Indians with whites and blacks), but this consoling fact does not present itself in contemplating the Antilles. Such was the state of society there, at the beginning of the sixteenth century, that the colonists did not mix with the natives, as do the English in Canada, except in rare instances.

The Indians of Cuba have disappeared like the Guanches of the Canary Islands, although in Guanabacoa, and in Teneriffe, within forty years, we have seen some fallacious pretences renewed, by which many families drew small pensions from the government, under the pretext that Indian, or Guanche blood circulated in their veins. No means now exist to arrive at a knowledge of the population of Cuba, or Haiti, in the time of Columbus; but how can we admit what some, in other respects judicious historians, state, that when the island of Cuba was conquered in 1511, it contained a million inhabitants, of whom 14,000 only remained in 1517? The statistical information which we find in the writings of the bishop of Chiàpa (Las Casas), is filled with contradictions, and if it be true that the good Dominican friar, Luis Bertram (who was persecuted by the grantees, as the Methodists in our days are by some English planters), predicted, on his return to

Spain, that "the 200,000 Indians now in the island of Cuba, will perish, victims to the cruelty of the Europeans," we must conclude that between the years 1555 and 1567, the indigenous race was far from being exterminated. Yet, according to Gomara (such is the confusion of the historians of that time), there was not one Indian in Cuba after 1553.

That we may form some idea of the vague character of the estimates made by the early Spanish voyagers, at a time when no knowledge existed of the population of a single province in Spain, we need only recur to the fact that the number of inhabitants which Captain Cook and other navigators estimated for Tahiti and the Sandwich Islands, varies from one to five, and that, too, at a period when statistics afforded exact means of comparison. It is easily perceived that Cuba, surrounded with banks abounding in fish, and having an extremely fertile soil, might have maintained many millions of those Indians, who were so abstemious that they did not taste of flesh, and cultivated only corn, yuca, and other alimentary roots. But had the population been so great, would it not have evinced a more advanced civilization than is revealed in the narrative of Columbus? Were the inhabitants of Cuba less civilized than those of the Lucayo Islands?

However active we may suppose the destructive

causes to have been, the cruelty of the conquerors, the brutality of the governors, the too severe labors of the gold washings, the ravages of the small pox, and the frequency of suicide, we can hardly conceive how, in thirty or forty years, I will not say a million, but even three or four hundred thousand Indians could become entirely extinct. The war with the cacique Hatuey was of short duration, and confined entirely to the eastern part of the island. Few complaints were made against the administration of the first two Spanish governors, Diego Velasquez and Pedro de Barba. The oppression of the natives began in the year 1539, with the arrival of the cruel Hernando de Soto.[1] Supposing Gomara to be correct in stating that there were no Indians fifteen years later, when Diego de Majariegos was governor (1554-1564), we must suppose that those who escaped to Florida in their pirogues,

---

[1] The researches of Don Juan Bantista de Muñoz, in the archives of Seville, have shown that cruelty to the Indians began very soon after the conquest. The revolting atrocities committed by Vasco Porcalla, in 1521, are cited by Sagra, and as early as 1534, the Cuban officials, in their letters to the emperor, asked for "7,000 negroes, that they might become inured to labor before the Indians ceased to exist." The mania of suicide to escape the labor imposed upon them, was common among the Indians long before the time of Hernando de Soto.—(See Sagra, *Historia Fisica, Politica y Natural*, large 8vo. Apend. pp. 8-26.)

believing, as tradition tells us, that they were return-
ing to the land of their ancestors, must have comprised a very considerable remnant of the population.
The mortality observed among the negro slaves in the
Antilles, in our days, may throw some light on these
contradictory statements.

Cuba must have seemed very populous to Columbus and Velasquez, if it was as well populated as
when the English landed in 1762. Early voyagers
are easily deceived by appearances, because they
estimate the population from the numbers of people
that the apparition of European vessels brings down
to the shore. But we know that the island of Cuba,
with the same towns and villages that it now possesses, did not contain over 200,000 inhabitants, in
1762; and even in a country where the people are
treated like slaves, exposed to brutal masters, to
excessive labor, ill-fed, and subject to the ravages of
the small pox, forty-two years are not sufficient that
the land should retain only the memory of their misfortunes. In many of the Lesser Antilles, which are
held by the English, population diminishes at the
rate of five or six per cent., annually; and in Cuba,
more than eight per cent.; but the entire destruction,
in forty-two years, of two hundred thousand, sup-
poses an annual loss of twenty-six per cent., which is
incredible, although we suppose the mortality of the

Indians to have been much greater than that of negro slaves, purchased at high prices.[1]

In studying the history of Cuba, we perceive that the movement of colonization has been from east to west, and that there, as in all the Spanish colonies, the regions first settled are those which are now least populous. The first settlement of the whites occurred in 1511, when the *Poblador y Conquistador* Velasquez, under orders from Don Diego Columbus, landed at Puerto de las Palmas, near Cape Maysi, then called Alpha and Omega, and subjugated the Cacique Hatuey, who had fled from Haiti to the eastern part of Cuba, where he became the chief of a confederation of several smaller native princes. In 1512 the city of Baracoa was founded, and soon afterwards St. Jago de Cuba (1514), Bayamo, Trinidad, Santi Espiritu, and Havana. The latter city was founded in 1515, on the southern coast of the island, in the partido of Güines, and four years later, was transferred to the Puerto de Carenas, the position of which, near the entrance of the two Bahama channels (the old and the new), seemed much more favorable for commerce than the coast southeast of Batabanó.

---

[1] Thus in the Spanish version, and in the original French. It is manifestly an arithmetical error.

Since the sixteenth century, the progress of the country has had a powerful influence on the relations of the several classes of population to each other, which vary in the grazing districts, and in those where the country has been long since cleared; in the seaports and in the country towns; in the districts where the colonial staples are planted, and in those which produce corn, vegetables and forage.

I. The district of Havana experiences a decrease in the relative white population of the capital, and its vicinity, but not in the interior towns, nor in the entire *Vuelta de Abajo*, where the tobacco plant is cultivated by free labor. In 1791, the census of Don Luis de las Casas gave to the district of Havana 137,800 souls, in which the proportion of whites, free colored, and slaves were as 53 : 20 : 27. More recently, in 1811, when the importations of slaves were very large, these proportions were estimated as 46 : 12 : 42.

In the districts containing the large plantations of sugar and coffee, which are the districts of great agricultural labor, the whites form barely one-third of the population, and the proportions of class (taking this expression in the sense of the proportion of each to the total population), oscillates, for the whites, between 30 and 36; for the free colored, between 3 and 6; and for the slaves, between 58 and

67 ; while in the districts of the *Vuelta de Abajo*, where tobacco is grown, it is found to be as 62 : 24 : 14 ; and in the grazing districts even, as 66 : 20 : 14. From these calculations, it would seem that where slavery exists, the proportion of free persons diminishes as population and refinement advance.

[NOTE.—The relative proportions of class in the several districts here cited by Baron Humboldt, are stated as follows, in the censuses of 1841 and 1846 :

	1841.	1846.
Western department,..	39 : 10 : 51	46 : 12 : 42
Sugar district,........	39 : 6 : 55	34 : 5 : 61
Tobacco district,......	57 : 12 : 31	54 : 16 : 30
Grazing do.	59 : 15 : 26	57 : 18 : 25

By this table, we perceive that the law of proportion exhibits nearly the same relative numbers stated by Baron Humboldt, and that the relative proportions have slightly changed, with the increased wealth of the island. We have elsewhere stated our want of confidence in the returns of 1846, and the above table indicates where they may err in their stated decrease of the slave population. While this has not decreased in the sugar, tobacco, or grazing districts, the returns for the whole department show a diminution in the total number of slaves. The capitation tax laid on house servants, in 1844, affords a partial reason for these diminished returns.]

II. The progress of population is more exactly known in the central and eastern portions of the island, than in the western department. That of the Cuatro Villas district has resulted from another class of industry. In Santi Espiritu, where the grazing *haciendas* increase, and in San Juan de los Remedios, where an active contraband trade is carried on with the Bahama Islands, the proportion of whites has increased between the years 1791 and 1811; while in the eminently fertile district of Trinidad, where the sugar culture has increased in an extraordinary degree, it has diminished.

[NOTE.—The law of population here expressed, still obtains in these districts. In 1841 the relative proportions of white, free colored, and slaves, were—

Santi Espiritu .... 65 : 15 : 20

Remedios .... 63 : 20 : 17

Trinidad .... 37 : 22 : 41.]

III. In the district of Puerto Principe the entire population has been nearly doubled in twenty years, and the white has increased eighty-nine per cent., as in the best portion of the United States. Yet the vicinity of Puerto Principe is nothing more than vast plains, where half wild cattle are pastured. The proprietors, says a modern traveller, are only assiduous to put in their chests the money brought by the overseers from their cattle-farms, from whence they bring it forth only for the purposes of play, or to carry on law-suits which have been handed down from generation to generation.

[NOTE.—Amid the general prosperity of Cuba, this district now presents the anomaly of a constantly decreasing population, the returns of the last three censuses being as follows :—

	Whites.	Free colored.	Slaves.
1827	39,375	6,911	15,704
1841	30,104	7,599	13,383
1846	23,006	7,403	10,827

We have never been able to obtain a satisfactory explanation of this fact; perhaps it may arise from the low ratio of profit from the grazing farms, when compared with other branches of labor, and the want of roads and means of communication in the district, which have combined to cause the population to remove to more favored localities. The recent completion of a railroad from the city of Principe to the port of Nuevitas, and a newly-awakened spirit of enterprise among the landed

11

proprietors, will, it is hoped, change this state of things.]

IV. In the district of St. Jago de Cuba, considered as a whole, the proportions of the different classes have experienced little alteration during the last twenty years. The partido of Bayamo is notable for the large number of free colored (44 per cent.), which increases yearly, as also in Holguin and Baracoa. In the vicinity of St. Jago the coffee plantations prosper and show a very considerable increase in the slaves.

[NOTE.—The law of population in this department has experienced little change since the time of Baron Humboldt's researches, with the exception of the district of Holguin. This district, situate on the north side of Cuba, possesses a very large stretch of the best agricultural lands, while its fine harbors, and clear coast, make it easily accessible to commerce. It has entered upon a career of agricultural labor, that holds out the most golden promise of reward; and the law of its population begins to assimilate to that of the Western department, which it may rival in agricultural prosperity.]

In the official documents published at Havana, an attempt has been made to compare the density of the population with that of the least populous portions of France and Spain. As the true area of the island was not then ascertained, these calculations have been inexact. We have already seen that the whole island has nearly two hundred inhabitants to the square league (in 1825); this is one-fourth less than Cuenca, the least populous province of Spain, and four times less than the higher Alpes, the least populous department of France.[1]

---

[1] Estimating the present population of Cuba by the *pro ratâ* of increase shown by the censuses of 1827 and 1841, the number and density of inhabitants at the close of 1855 is approximately as follows:—

Department.	Population.	Area, Square Miles.	Density.
Western	966,000	8,077	120
Central	280,000	14,898	16
Eastern	200,000	11,258	22
Total	1,446,000	34,233	42

Making the present density about 378 inhabitants to the square league. The density of the Western department approximates very nearly to that of Massachusetts; that of the Central department to Georgia; and that of the Eastern to Tennessee, as exhibited by the census of 1850. The number of inhabitants to the square mile in the principal countries of Europe, is as follows:—

Belgium, ... 388		Prussia, ... 151	
England, ... 822		Austria, ... 142	
Holland, ... 259		Denmark, ... 102	
France, ... 173		Portugal, ... 95	
Switzerland, ... 160		Spain, ... 78	

The population of Cuba is so unequally distributed, that we may consider five-sixths of the island as uninhabited. There are several parishes (Consolacion, Macuriges, Hanabana), in which there are barely fifteen inhabitants to the square league; while, on the other hand, in the triangle between Bahia Honda, Batabanó, and Matanzas (or, more correctly stated, between the Pan of Guajaibon, Batabanó, and Guamacaro), there are 300,000 inhabitants in 410 square leagues, or in one-ninth of the total area of the island; this is three-sevenths of its population, and six-sevenths of its agricultural and commercial wealth. Yet this triangle contains only 782 inhabitants to the square league, its extent being somewhat less than that of two of the medium departments of France, and its density of population one-half smaller. We should remember, that even in this small triangle between Guajaibon, Batabanó, and Guamacaro, the southern portion is entirely uninhabited.

The least populous parishes, containing only grazing farms, are those of Santa Cruz de los Pinos, Guanacape, Cacaragicaras, Pinal del Rio, Guane, and Baja, in the *Vuelta de Abajo*, and Macuriges, Hanabana, Guamacaro, and Alvarez, in the *Vuelta de Arriba*.[1] The *hatos* (large cattle farms), with

---

[1] These districts of the *Vuelta de Arriba* have now become the

1,600 or 1,800 caballerias of uncultivated land, are gradually disappearing; and, if the new settlements at Guantanamo and Nuevitas have not experienced the rapid growth which had been anticipated, others, as for instance that of Guanajay, have been very prosperous. (*Expediente de Don Francisco de Arango*, 1798, *MSS.*) In the preceding pages, I have stated with what facility the population of Cuba may increase in future years. Being myself a native of the cold North, that partakes in a small degree of Nature's bounty, I remember that the mark of Bradenburg, which is in a great degree sandy, maintains, thanks to an administration favorable to agriculture and industry, a population twice greater than that of Cuba, on an area three times smaller than hers.

The unequal distribution of the population, the want of inhabitants on a great part of the coasts, together with the great extent of these, make the military defence of the island an impossibility; for, neither the contraband trade, nor the debarcation of an enemy can be prevented. Havana is, undoubtedly, a strongly fortified place, its works rivalling

great seat of the sugar culture, and are both populous and prosperous. They are intimately connected with Havana, and with the ports of Matanzas and Cardenas, by a well-devised system of railway.

those of the most important cities of Europe; the
small towers and forts of Cojima, Jaruco, Matanzas,
Mariel, Bahia Honda, Batabanó, Jagua, and Trinidad, may offer a longer or shorter resistance, but
nearly two-thirds of the island has no defence whatever; for however active the service of gun-boats
may be, it could never be of much importance.

Intellectual cultivation, limited entirely to the
whites, is distributed with the same inequality as the
population. The intercourse of the best society of
Havana resembles, in its polite forms and urbanity,
that of Cadiz and the richest commercial cities of
Europe; but as we leave the capital, and its neighboring plantations inhabited by wealthy planters, we
notice the contrast presented by a state of partial
and local civilization, with the simple habits and
customs that obtain in the small towns and isolated
haciendas.

The Habaneros have been the first among the
rich Spanish colonists to travel in Spain, France,
and Italy. Nowhere are the politics of Europe,
and the springs which sustain or overturn a ministry, better understood than in Havana. This knowledge of passing events, and a foresight of the future,
have been of great advantage to the inhabitants of
Cuba, in freeing them from the difficulties which
delay the advance of colonial prosperity. In the

interval of time elapsed from the peace of the Versailles to the revolution of St. Domingo, Havana has seemed ten times nearer to Spain than Mexico, Caraccas, or New Granada. During my residence in the colonies, fifteen years later, this apparent inequality had already become greatly diminished. At the present time, when the independence of the continental colonies, the importation of the products of foreign industry, and the outflow of the coinage of the new States, have increased the intercourse between Europe and America; when distance is so much diminished by improvements in navigation, and the inhabitants of Mexico, Colombia, and Guatemala, rival each other in visiting Europe, the greater part of the old colonies of Spain, at least those washed by the Atlantic, seem also to be much nearer to our continent.

Such are the changes produced in a few years, and which are extending in an extraordinary degree, by the diffusion of knowledge, and by an activity which had been long repressed, that the contrasts of manners and civilization, which I had observed in the beginning of the present century, in Caraccas, Bogotá, Quito, Lima, Mexico, and Habana, have become less apparent. The influence of the original Basques, Catalans, Gallegos, and Andalusians is daily becoming less; and at this time it would be, perhaps, unjust to draw the distinctions of national refinement in the six capitals I have just named, as I had intended doing in another place.

The island of Çuba has no great and sumptuous establishments, whose foundation dates from a time long anterior to those of Mexico; but Havana possesses institutions which the patriotism of the inhabitants, stimulated by a praiseworthy rivalry with the other centres of American civilization, may enlarge and perfect, when political affairs and public confidence in the preservation of domestic repose shall permit it.[1]

The Patriotic Society of Havana (founded in 1793), those of Santi Espiritu, Trinidad, and Puerto Principe, which are branches of that at Havana;[2] the University, with its professorships of Theology, Jurisprudence, Medicine,[3] and Mathematics, founded in 1728, in the

---

[1] This was written at a time when the Congress of American nations at Panama, and the conspiracy of the "Soles de Bolivar" in Cuba, inspired serious doubts of the stability of the Spanish power there.

[2] These societies were suppressed a few years since, and their functions merged in the Junta de Fomento.

[3] In 1825, there were, in Havana alone, more than 500 licensed physicians, 333 surgeons, *latinos y romancistas* (surgeons and barbers), and 100 apothecaries. At the same time, there were, in the whole island, 312 lawyers (of which, 198 were in Havana), and 94 notaries. The number of lawyers has greatly increased since 1814, when there were only 98 in Havana, and 130 in all the island.—H.

Dominican monastery;[1] the chair of Political Economy, established in 1818, of Agricultural Botany, the School of Descriptive Anatomy and Museum, due to the enlightened zeal of Don Alejandro Ramirez, the public Library, the Free School of Drawing and Painting, the Nautical Academy, the Lancasterian schools, and the Botanical Garden, are noble institutions, partly new and partly old, some of which are susceptible and worthy of improvement, and others need a complete reform to bring them into harmony with the wants of society and the spirit of the age.

[1] The clergy of Cuba is neither numerous nor rich, excepting the bishop of Havana, and the archbishop of Cuba; the first has $110,000, and the latter $40,000 annual income.* The prebendaries have $3,000 a year. The number of ecclesiastics does not exceed 1,100, as appears by the official census which I possess.—H.

* This has been greatly diminished by the expropriation of the church property.

.

CHAPTER VIII.

SUGAR CULTURE.

Historical summary—Export of sugar from Havana to 1824—
From Cuba to 1852—Estimates of actual product—Wealth of
Cuba compared with the Antilles—St. Domingo—Brazil—Effect
of political disasters on prices—Relative position of Cuba—
Classes of sugar—Numerical elements of sugar planting—Value
of land—Number of hands to a plantation, and their food—Machinery—Cost, product, and expense of a sugar plantation in 1825.
[NOTE—In 1855—Compared—Causes of increased product.]—
Mean yield of land in sugar-cane, maple, and beet—Proportions of
crystallizable sugar—Different results in manipulations of cane-
juice—Where improvements must be sought—Yield of cane in
new and old lands—Compared with wheat—Yield in Bengal—
Disproportion of results in agriculture in Cuba and France—First
beet-root sugar in Havana—Fears entertained—Changes in sugar
culture—Increase—First cane planted in America—Several classes
—Supposition of sugar-makers—Otaheitan cane has not degenerated
—Want of fuel—Application of bagass—Wood and bagass compared—Experiments and inventions—Suggested by the author's
residence at salt-works—Error in Europe relative to the effect of
cessation of slave-trade—Number of slaves in sugar culture—In
towns—Capture of Havana by the English, and its good effects—
Causes of prosperity—Evils of government embarrass it.

WHEN the Spaniards first settled in the islands,
and on the continent of America, they began, as in

Europe, to cultivate the principal articles necessary
for the sustenance of man. This system of agricultural life among the people, is the most natural, and
is that which inspires society with the greatest confidence, and it has been preserved in Mexico, Peru,
and the temperate and cold regions of Cundina-
marca, where the power of the whites has extended
over a vast expanse of country. Several alimentary
plants, as the plantain, yuca, maize, the cereals of
Europe, and the potato, have been, at different
elevations above the level of the sea, the basis of
continental agriculture within the tropics. Indigo,
cotton, coffee, and the sugar-cane, are found only in
scattered groups in those countries.

The same was the case in Cuba, and the other
islands of the Antilles, for two and a half centuries.
The same plants which had served to maintain the
half-savage Indian, were cultivated there, and the
vast plains of the larger islands were filled with
numerous herds of cattle. In 1520 Pedro de Atienza
planted the first sugar-cane in St. Domingo, and rude
cylinder presses, moved by water-power, are still
constructed there. Cuba participated very slightly
in this new industry, and it is most singular that the
historians of the conquest, at as late a period as
1553, do not speak of any other export of sugar to
Spain and Peru, than that of Mexico. Havana, far

from contributing to commerce what we now style colonial staples, exported only hides and skins, until the eighteenth century.

The cultivation of tobacco and the care of bees, the first hives of which were carried from Florida, succeeded the raising of cattle. Wax and tobacco were soon more important articles of commerce than hides, and were in their turn, superseded by sugar and coffee. The cultivation of these articles did not diminish that of the former ones, and in these different phases of agricultural industry, notwithstanding the efforts we have seen to make the coffee culture predominate, the sugar plantations have thus far yielded the greatest returns. The export, through licit and illicit channels, of coffee, tobacco, sugar, and wax, has risen to fourteen millions annually, estimated at the present value of those staples.

The export of sugar from Havana alone during the last sixty-four years, according to the custom-house returns, is as follows :—

From 1760 to 1763, average at most...... 13,000 Boxes.
"   1770 " 1780..................... 50,000 "

1786, ...	63,274 Boxes.	1791, ...	85,014 "
1787,....	61,245 "	1792,....	72,854 "
1788,....	69,221 "	1793,. ..	87,970 "
1789,....	69,125 "	1794,....103,629 "
1790,. ..	77,896 "	1795,....	70,437 "

1796,... 120,374 Boxes.		1804,....193,955 Boxes.	
1797,....118,066	"	1805,....174,544	"
1798,....134,872	"	1806, ...156,510	"
1799,....165,602	"	1807,....181,272	"
1800, ...142,097	"	1808,....125,875	"
1801,....159,841	"	1809,....238,842	"
1802,....204,404	"	1810,....186,672	"
1803,....158,073	"		

From 1811 to 1814 average yearly ....206,487 "

1815,....214,111	"	1820,....215,593	"
1816,....200,487	"	1821,....236.669	"
1817,....217,076	"	1822,....261,795	"
1818,....207.378	"	1823,....300.211	"
1819,....192,743	"	1824,....245,329	"

This table, which is the most complete that has been published up to the present time, is based upon a great number of manuscript official documents, which have been communicated to me; on the *Aurora*, and *Papel Periodico* of Havana; the *Patriota Americano;* the *Guias de forasteros* of Cuba; the *Sucinta Noticia de la situacion presente de la Habana*, 1800, MSS.; *Reclamacion contra la ley de Aranceles*, 1821; and the *Redactor General* of Guatemala, July 1825, p. 25.

[1] According to the official returns, the export of sugar from Cuba, since 1824, has been as follows:

1825	488,776 Boxes.	
1826 to 1830...............................	2,083,798	"
1831 " 1835	2,486,492	"

In order to arrive at the exact export of sugar
from Cuba, we must add to the exports from Havana;
1st. That of the other open ports, particularly Matanzas, St. Jago de Cuba, Trinidad, Baracoa, and Mariel;
and 2d. The amount of contraband commerce.
During my stay in the island, the export of Trinidad
was estimated at 25,000 boxes. In examining the
custom-house returns of Matanzas, we must avoid
the repetition of amounts, and carefully distinguish
between the sugar exported directly to Europe, and
that shipped to Havana. In 1819, the real trans-
Atlantic export from Matanzas did not exceed one-
thirteenth of that from Havana, and in 1823 I found
it to be one-tenth. According to these data, we
may add to the 235,000 boxes, which is the mean
term of export from Havana alone for the last eight
years (in 1825), at least 70,000 boxes shipped from
other ports; so that (estimating the frauds in the
custom-house at one-fourth), the total export of the
island is more than 380,000 boxes of sugar yearly.

Well-informed persons estimated the consumption

1886 to 1840	8,171,428	Boxes.
1841 " 1845	4,024,405	"
1846 " 1850	4,840,768	"
1851	1,589,994	"
1852	1,409,012	"

No official returns of the commerce of the island, since 1852, have
been published.

of Havana, in 1794, at 18,600 boxes, and 45,600 that of all the island. In view of the fact that the population of the island at that time was about 362,000, of which, at most, only 230,000 were free, and that it is now 715,000, of which 455,000 are free, we must estimate a total consumption in 1825, of 88,000 boxes. But supposing it to be 60,000 boxes, we have a total product of at least 440,000 boxes from the sugar plantations.

That we may more exactly comprehend the agricultural wealth of Cuba, let us compare the production of that island in moderately productive years, with that of the other Antilles.[1]

SLAVE POPULATION AND EXPORT OF SUGAR IN 1823.

	Slaves.	Export.
Cuba,	260,000	1,520,000 cwt.
Jamaica,	342,382	1,417,488
Barbadoes, Granada, and St. Vincent,	128,000	794,567
Trinidad,	23,500	189,891
All the English Antilles,	626,800	3,005,366
French Antilles,	178,000	794,760
Dutch, Danish, and Swedish Antilles,	61,300	354,386

[1] We have here reduced Baron Humboldt's extended remarks to the tabular form, for greater conciseness. The export of sugar from Cuba, in 1851, had increased to six millions hundred weight, while that of all the English West Indies had fallen to about 2,750,000 hundred weight.

The present export from St. Domingo is very insignificant. In 1788 it amounted to 80,360,000 kilogrammes, and in 1799 it was still estimated to reach twenty millions kilogrammes. If it had been maintained as in the time of its greatest prosperity, it would augment the export of sugar of all the Antilles 28 per cent. and that of all America 18 per cent. Brazil, Guiana, and Cuba together, with their 2,526,000 slaves, supply (in 1825) nearly 230,000,000 kilogrammes; that is to say, exclusive of contraband, three times more sugar than St. Domingo, at the time of its greatest prosperity. The great increase of product in Brazil, Demarara, and Cuba, has replaced the loss of Haiti, and made the destruction of the sugar industry of that island less sensible.

The production of Brazil, which contains 1,960,000 slaves, and where the sugar-cane is cultivated from the district of Rio Grande to the parallel of Puerto Alegre (30° 2' S. lat.), is much greater than is generally supposed. In 1816 it was, according to very exact data, 200,000 boxes, of 650 kilogrammes each, or 130,000,000 kilogrammes (about 650,000 cwt.). The production of sugar in this country has diminished greatly since 1816, in consequence of domestic disturbances, and in years of great drought has barely reached 140,000 boxes. Those who are conversant with this branch of American commerce, believe that when tranquillity has been reëstablished, the mean annual export of sugar will reach 192,000 boxes.[1]

Equinoctial America and Louisiana yield annually (in 1825), to the commerce of Europe and America, as appears by a minute comparison of all the partial statistics, 460,000,000 kilogrammes of sugar, as follows:—

Antilles,....1,147,500 slaves, 287, or 62 per cent.
Brazil,......2,060.000 " 125, " 27 " "
Guiana, ...206,000 " 40, " 9 " "

Great Britain alone, with a population of 14,400,000, consumes more than one-third part of the 460,000,000 kilogrammes supplied by those countries of the new continent, where the slave-trade has gathered 3,314,000 unfortunate slaves.

The cultivation of the sugar cane is now so widely extended in different parts of the world, that any physical or political causes which might suspend, or destroy industrial labor in one of the great Antilles, would not affect the price of sugar, nor exercise that influence in the general trade of Europe and America they would have exercised when the great cultivation was concentrated in a smaller space. Spanish

[1] The product of sugar in Brazil, in 1851, amounted to 117,000 tons of 2,000 lbs. each.—*Hunt's Merchant's Magazine.*

writers have often compared the island of Cuba, from
the wealth of its productions, with the mines of Guanajuato in Mexico. And in truth, Guanajuato, at the
beginning of the nineteenth century, supplied one-
fourth part of all the silver from Mexico, and one-sixth
of that from all America. Cuba exports at this time
(1825), through licit channels, one-fourth of the
sugar from all the Antilles, and one-eighth of all the
sugar that goes from equinoctial America to Europe
and the United States.

In Cuba there are four qualities of sugar, according to its purity or degree of purging. Of each loaf,
or cone with the base uppermost, the upper part
gives white sugar, the middle gives brown, and the
lower, or point of the cone gives *cucurucho;* these
three grades of Cuba sugar are purged, and but a
small portion is manufactured as raw, or *moscabado*
sugar. As the purging forms are of different size,
the loaf varies in weight; it is usually about twenty-
five pounds after being purged. The sugar masters
desire that each loaf should give $\frac{4}{7}$ of white, $\frac{2}{7}$ of
brown, and $\frac{1}{7}$ of *cucurucho* sugar.

During my residence in the plain of Güines, I
endeavored to gather some exact data relative to
the numerical elements of sugar-cane planting. A
large sugar plantation producing from 2,000 to 2,500
boxes, generally has fifty *caballerias* of land (about

1,600 acres), one-half of which is planted in cane, and the other is appointed for alimentary plants and pastures, which latter are called *potreros*. The value of the land naturally varies according to its quality, and vicinity to the ports of Havana, Matanzas, or Mariel. In a radius of twenty-five leagues around Havana, the value of each *caballeria* may be estimated at two or three thousand dollars.[1]

That a plantation may produce 2,000 boxes of sugar, it must have three hundred negroes.[2] An adult male slave, who is acclimated, is worth 450 or 500 dollars, and an unacclimated, newly imported African, 870 tó 400 dollars. A negro costs from 45 to 50 dollars a year in food, clothing, and medicine,

[1] The land measure known as a *caballeria*, is a square, having 18 *cordels*, each *cordel* being 24 *varas*, or 432 *varas* of a side; consequently, a *caballeria* has 186,624 square *varas*, equivalent to 82 1-10 English acres.—H.

[2] There are very few plantations in Cuba that make 2,500 boxes; only those of Rio Blanco, of the Marquis de Arcos, of Don Rafael O'Farril, and Doña Felicia Jauregui, attain this quantity. Those which produce 2,000 boxes, annually, are considered first class sugar plantations.—H.

There has been a great change in this respect, since Baron Humboldt wrote, and a large number of the plantations in the Western department yield from 4,000 to 5,000 boxes, annually. A first class sugar plantation in Cuba now yields from 7,500 to 10,000 boxes, annually.

consequently, including the interest on capital, and throwing off the holidays, the cost of labor is a little more than twenty-five cents a day. The slaves are supplied with jerked beef from Buenos Ayres and Caraccas, and salt fish, when meat is dear; with vegetables, such as plantains, pumpkins, sweet potatoes, potatoes, and corn. In the year 1804, jerked beef was worth 5 to 6 cents a pound in Güines, and in 1825, its cost is from 7 to 8 cents.

On a sugar plantation such as we are describing, producing 2,000 or 2,500 boxes of sugar, there are required, 1st, three cylinder mills, worked by oxen or water-power; 2d, eighteen kettles, according to the old Spanish method, which, having a very slow fire, burns much wood; and according to the French method, introduced in 1801, by Bailli, from St. Domingo, under the auspices of Don Nicolas Calvo, three clarifiers, three large kettles, and two boiling trains (each having three boilers), in all, twelve pieces. It is generally said that seventy-five pounds of purged sugar yields one keg (seven gallons) of molasses; and that this, with the refuse sugar, covers the expenses of the plantation; but this can be true only where large quantities of rum are made. Two thousand boxes of sugar give 15,000 kegs of molasses, which will make 500 pipes of rum, worth $25 each.

If we form a table of product and expenditure from these data, we find—

2,000 Boxes Sugar (white and brown), at $24,	....	$48,000
500 Pipes of Rum, at $25,	....	12,500
		$60,500

The yearly expenses of the plantation are estimated at.................. .... $30,000

The capital invested consists of

50 caballerias of land, at $2,500,	....	$125,000
300 negroes, at $450,	....	135,000
Buildings, mills, &c.,	....	80,000
Cattle, and general inventory,	....	130,000
		$470,000

From this estimate, we find that if a plantation capable of producing 2,000 boxes is established, the capitalist would receive 6½ per cent. interest, according to the old Spanish method, and the present prices of sugar. This return is not exorbitant for an establishment that is not purely agricultural, and whose expenditures are always the same, even though the return should fall off one-third. We need not be surprised, therefore, that the cultivation of rice should be preferred in Cuba to that of sugar, when the price of the latter is so low as 4 or 5 cents a pound.

The profit of a plantation, established some time since, consists in, 1st, the fact that, twenty years since, the cost of making a plantation was much less than now; for, a *caballeria* of good land cost then only $1,200 or $1,600, instead of $2,000 or $2,500, as now; and an adult negro $300, instead of $450 to $500; and, 2d, the variable returns—the prices of sugar having been at times very low, and at others very high. The prices of sugar have varied so much, during a period of ten years, that the return on the capital invested has varied from five to fifteen per cent.

[NOTE.—That the reader may compare the state of the sugar industry, at the present time, with the foregoing clear statement of its numerical elements, we insert here the estimates presented in an able and lucid work on the political and economical condition of Cuba, printed during the present year, 1855, for private circulation. It is from the pen of a gentleman distinguished alike for his literary attainments, his ability as a sugar planter and economist, and his disinterested zeal for the welfare of his native land. He says:

" We select a plantation producing 4,000 boxes, which is neither one of the colossal ones recently made, nor one of those deemed small.

300 negroes of both sexes and various ages
at $600,............................ $180,000
34 *caballerias* of land, in cane, at $2,500,.. 85,000
6 *caballerias* of land, at $2,000,......... 12,000
Steam engine and cane mills, ... 16,000
Buildings,........... 35,500
Boiling trains, &c.,...................... 15,000
————————
$343,500

Less—First value of land, which remains on
ground rent, $600 a *caballeria*,.... 24,000
————————
$319,500

4,000 boxes of sugar, average, $16, ... $64,000
Product of molasses sold,................. 6,000
————————
$70,000

The yearly expenses of the plantation are estimated, inclusive of an annual purchase of
cattle at. $36,110
Repairs and replacing material, ... 14,600
————————
$50,710

leaving a profit of $19,290, being a return of 6½ per
cent. on the capital invested."

The number of hands on the plantation is the
same in both estimates, and there is one-fifth less
land in the modern than in the old plantation, while
the product of sugar is exactly double. This great
difference of yield arises, in part, from the following
circumstances, and in part, perhaps, from improve-

ments in the mode of culture, and of expressing the juice from the cane. The able writer I have just quoted estimates that the improved division of labor, the use of steam-power, the introduction of mechanical appliances, as railway from the boiling-house to the purging-house, pumps for several purposes, and water pipes, improved furnaces and clarifiers, cane carriers, bagass-carts, &c., and the greater facilities of transition to market, make an actual saving of seventy-nine hands to the plantation.

This largely increases the number of hands that can be applied to field labor, and consequently increases the breadth of land in cane, while the use of steam-power, and a small increase in the capacity of the boiling trains, suffices for the purpose of manufacture. Such is the magical influence of the improved mechanical appliances of our day, upon the product of man's labor. Great improvements have also been effected in the chemical processes of sugar-making; but their effect is, perhaps, experienced more in the improved quality, than in the greater quantity of sugar produced. The sugar planters of Cuba, as a class, are exceedingly intelligent, and quick to adopt improvements in their system of labor.]

From calculations which I made, when in Cuba, I

have estimated that a *hectar* of cane gives a mean
of twelve cubic metres of juice, from which are
extracted, by the method at present in use, at most,
ten or twelve per cent. of raw sugar. Considering,
therefore, the juice as a liquid charged with salts, it
contains, according to the fertility of the soil, from
twelve to sixteen per cent. of crystallizable sugar.
The sugar maple, in good lands in the United States,
yields 450 grammes of sugar to eighteen kilogrammes of sap, being two and a half per cent. The
same quantity of sugar is yielded by the beet root,
comparing this quantity with the entire weight of
root. Twenty thousand kilogrammes of beets, grown
in good land, yield five hundred kilogrammes of
raw sugar.

As the sugar cane loses one-half its weight, when
the juice is expressed, it gives—comparing, not the
product of juices, but the root of the common beet
with the sugar cane—six times more raw sugar, to
an equal weight of vegetable matter, than the beet
root. The juice of the cane varies in its constituent
parts, according to the nature of the soil, the quantity of rain, the distribution of heat in the different
seasons, and the earlier or later disposition of the
plant to flower. It is not alone in the greater or less
quantity of sugar held in solution, as some sugar-
makers suppose; the difference consists rather in the

12

proportions of crystallizable and uncrystallizable sugar, albumen, gum, green fecula, and malic acid.

The quantity of crystallizable sugar may be the same, and yet, according to the operations used, the quantity of sugar extracted from an equal weight of juice, will vary considerably; this arises from the different connection between the other peculiar principles of crystallizable sugar. This sugar, on combining with some of the other principles, forms a syrup which does not possess the quality of crystallization, and remains in the refuse. A too great degree of heat seems to hasten and increase the loss. These considerations explain the reason why the sugar-makers sometimes, at certain seasons of the year, consider themselves bewitched, because, with the same applications, they cannot make the same quantity of sugar. They also explain why the same juice, under modified operations—for instance, the degrees of heat, and the rapidity of boiling—yields more or less sugar.

It has been said, and I again repeat it, that we must not look for great improvements in the manufacture of sugar, from the construction or manner of setting the boilers and furnaces only, but from improvements in the chemical operations, a more intimate knowledge of the effect of lime, of alkaline substances, of animal carbon, and, lastly, in an exact

determination of the maximum heat to which the
juice should be exposed in the successive boilers.
The ingenious analysis of sugar, starch, gum, and the
ligneous principles, made by Messrs. Gay Lussac and
Thenard, the labors carried on in Europe with grape
and beet-root sugar, and the investigations of
Dutrone, Proust, Clarke, Higgins, Daniell, Howard,
Braconnot, and Derosne, have facilitated and prepared the attainment of these degrees of perfection;
but nothing has been done in the Antilles.

The amalgamation of metals, on a large scale, in
Mexico, cannot, certainly, be improved without a
previous examination, during a long stay at Guanajuato, or Real del Monte, of the nature of the
metals placed in contact with the mercury, the
muriate of soda, lime, &c.; in the same manner, to
improve the technical manipulations on the sugar
plantations, we must begin on several of those in
Cuba, with an analysis by a chemist acquainted
with the present state of vegetable chemistry, of
small portions of juice taken from the several kinds
of cane, in different soils, and at various seasons of
the year. Without this preliminary labor, undertaken by some person from one of the most celebrated laboratories, and possessing a complete knowledge
of the operations of sugar-making from beet-root, we
may obtain some partial improvement, but the

manufacture of sugar will always continue to be what it now is, that is to say, the result of experiments more or less satisfactory, but which are made in the dark.

In the lands that can be irrigated, and those where tuberous roots have been grown before planting the cane, a *caballeria* of fertile land, instead of yielding 1,500 arrobes of sugar, will yield 3,000 or 4,000 arrobes, which is equal to 2,660 or 3,540 kilogrammes of white and brown sugar to the hectar.   Taking it at 1,500 arrobes, and estimating it at the price in Havana, of $24 a box, we find that a hectar of land will produce in value, $15 40 in sugar, and $5 76 in wheat, supposing an eight-fold yield, and a price of $3 60 per 100 kilogrammes.   I have stated elsewhere, that in comparing these two branches of agriculture, we must bear in mind that sugar-planting requires a very large capital; at present, for example, in order to produce 2,000 boxes in a single establishment, $400,000 are required.

In the irrigated lands of Bengal, an acre yields, according to Brockford and Roxburgh, 2,300 kilogrammes of raw sugar, which is equal to 5,700 kilogrammes to the hectar. This fertility being common to a large breadth of land in India, we need not be surprised at the low price of sugar there.   The yield

of a hectar is double what it is in the Antilles, and
the daily wages of an East Indian is one-third that
of a negro slave in Cuba.

. Supposing, as we should when we speak of the
production of all Cuba, that in lands of mean fertility a *caballeria* yields 1,500 arrobes of purged
sugar, we find that nineteen and three-fourths
square leagues (about one-ninth the area of one of
the medium departments of France), suffice to produce the 430,000 boxes of sugar which Cuba yields
for domestic use and exportation. It seems surprising that less than twenty square leagues of land can
give an annual product, whose value (estimating a
box of sugar in Havana at $24), exceeds $10,400,000.
In order to supply the 56 or 60 millions kilogrammes
of raw sugar, consumed by the thirty millions of
people in France, there would be required, within
the tropics, nine and five-sixths square leagues of
land cultivated in sugar-cane; in the temperate
zone, thirty-seven and a half leagues of land in beet-
root are necessary. A hectar of good land in
France, planted in beet-root, produces from ten
thousand to twenty thousand kilogrammes. The
average yield is twenty thousand kilogrammes, which
give 2½ per cent., or 500 kilogrammes of raw sugar.
One hundred kilogrammes of raw sugar yield fifty
kilogrammes of refined (30 of brown sugar and 20

of loaf); consequently, a hectar, in beet root, yields 250 kilogrammes of refined sugar.

Shortly before my arrival at Havana, some samples of beet root sugar were carried there from Germany, and this article was said "to menace the existence of the sugar-growing isles of America." The sugar-planters saw, not without some alarm, that it was a substance exactly like cane sugar; but they consoled themselves with the hope that the cost of the labor, and the difficulty of separating the crystallizable sugar from so large a mass of vegetable pulp, would make the operation expensive and profitless. Since that time chemistry has triumphed over these obstacles; for, in 1812, there were in France two hundred manufactories of sugar from the beet root, working with variable results, and producing a million kilogrammes of sugar, annually. But the inhabitants of the Antilles, well aware of what transpires in Europe, entertain now no fears of the beet root, grape, or chestnut sugar, nor of the coffee of Naples, or the indigo of the south of France.

The greatest changes which have been produced in the culture of the sugar cane, and the laboratories of the plantations, took place between the years 1796 and 1800. First, mules were substituted for oxen, as motive-power for the sugar mills; then

water-power was introduced in Güines, it having
been used even by the first settlers in St. Domingo;
and, finally, experiments with steam-power were
made at Ceibabo, by Count Jaruco y Mopox. There
are now twenty-five of these steam-engines on different estates in Cuba.[1] The cultivation of the Otaheitan cane is also becoming very general. Clarifiers,
and better arranged reverberating furnaces, have
been introduced. We must also confess, in honor of
the wealthy planters, that on a great number of
plantations, the greatest care is taken of the sick
slaves, of the children, and to increase the number
of women.

In 1775 the island contained 473 sugar plantations, and in 1817 there were more than 780. None
of the former produced even a fourth part of the
sugar that is now produced by a second-class plantation; it is not, therefore, the number of plantations
alone that will give us a true idea of the progress of
this branch of agricultural industry. The district of
Havana contained, in 1763, 70 sugar plantations; in
1796, 305; in 1806, 480; and in 1817, 625.[2]

[1] The census of 1846 states the number of sugar plantations with
steam-power at 286, since when the number has very largely
increased.

[2] The number in 1846 was 735. In 1850, the total number of
sugar plantations in Cuba exceeded 1750.

The first plant of cane in virgin soil, carefully planted, will continue to yield for twenty or twenty-three years, but, after that, it is necessary to replant every three years. On the hacienda Matamoros, there was, in 1804, a cane-field, which had been planted forty-five years. The most fertile sugar lands now under cultivation (1825) are those in the vicinity of Mariel and Guanajay. The variety of the sugar cane, known as Otaheitan cane, which is distinguishable at some distance by its deep green, yields, on the same lands, one-fourth more juice, and a larger and more woody fibre, and is consequently richer in combustible matter than any other variety.

The sugar-makers on the plantations, who have all the presumption of a little learning, pretend that the juice of the Otaheitan cane is worked more easily, and that it yields more crystallizable sugar, and less cane-juice potash than that of the other varieties. This south sea cane, after six or seven years' cultivation, certainly has a thinner rind, but the knots remain much further apart than in the creole cane. Fortunately the fears that were at first entertained, that the Otaheitan cane would degenerate into the ordinary sugar cane, have not been realized. In Cuba it is planted during the rainy months of July and October, and the crop is brought in from February to May.

As the forests of Cuba have disappeared, through excessive clearing of the land, the sugar plantations have begun to experience the want of fuel. In former times, a small portion of bagass (the crushed cane), had been used to enliven the boiling fires, under the old kettles, but it is only since the immigrants from St. Domingo introduced the reverberating furnace that the attempt to abandon wood, and burn only bagass has been made. In the old form of furnaces and kettles, a load of wood, of 160 cubic feet, is consumed to make five arrobes of sugar, so that for one hundred kilogrammes of raw sugar, 278 cubic feet of lemon and orange wood are required. With the reverberating furnace of St. Domingo, one load of bagass containing 495 cubic feet, made 640 pounds of raw sugar, which is equal to 158 cubic feet of bagass to 100 kilogrammes of sugar.

During my residence in Güines, and particularly at Rio Blanco, while at the house of the Count Jaruco y Mopox, I made experiments with several new constructions for the purpose of diminishing the amount of fuel, by surrounding the fire with substances that were bad conductors of heat, attaining, at the same time, greater protection to the negroes while feeding the fire. A long stay at the salt works in Europe, and the art of practical salt-making which I had learned in my youth, gave me

12*

the idea of those inventions, which have since been extended with some usefulness. Wooden covers placed on the clarifiers hastened the evaporation, and induced me to believe that a system of covers, and movable ladles suspended with counter-weights, might be usefully extended to the other kettles. This idea is worthy of examination, but we must graduate with care the quantity of syrup, the crystallizable sugar obtained, and that which is lost, the fuel, time, and pecuniary expense of the experiments.

An error has generally prevailed in Europe, which has had no small influence in the study of the effects a cessation of the African slave trade might produce, in supposing that in the so-called *sugar colonies* of the Antilles the greater part 'of the slaves are employed on the sugar estates. There is no doubt that the cultivation of the sugar cane is one of the most powerful stimulants of the slave-trade, but a very plain calculation proves, that the mass of slaves in the Antilles is three times greater than the number employed on the sugar plantations. Ten years since I stated, that if the 200,000 boxes of sugar, which Cuba exported in 1812, were made on the larger plantations, 30,000 slaves would suffice for that branch of industry.

It is estimated in Cuba that for the production of 1,000 boxes of clayed sugar, 150 negroes, on an average, are needed; consequently 440,000 boxes would require only 66,000 slaves. If to these were added 36,000, which are required in Cuba, in the cultivation of coffee and tobacco, we find that of the 260,000 slaves now there, barely 100,000 suffice for the three great staples of colonial industry, upon which is based its active commerce. On the other hand, the tobacco is cultivated almost entirely by whites and free blacks. I have said elsewhere, and I base my statement on the very respectable authority of the *Consulado* of Havana, that one-third part (32 per cent.) of the slaves live in the cities and large towns, and, therefore, take no part in the rural labors. If therefore, we take into consideration: 1*st*, the large number of children not yet able to work, scattered over the plantations; and, 2*d*, the necessity of employing a much larger number of negroes on the small and distant plantations, in order to produce an equal amount of sugar to that produced on the great plantations, we shall find that of 187,000 slaves in the rural districts, at least one-fourth part, or 46,000, produce neither sugar, coffee, nor tobacco.

I have stated that before the year 1762, Cuba contributed no more to commerce than is now done by the provinces of Veragua, Panama, and Darien, which, of the Spanish-American provinces, are the

least productive in agricultural products. An
event which was apparently a misfortune, the
capture of Havana by the English, awakened the
public mind. The city was evacuated by them on
the 6th July, 1763, and from that time we trace the
first efforts of a new-born industry.[1]

The construction of new fortifications on a gigan-
tic scale,[2] placed large sums of money in immediate
circulation, and the slave-trade, which was subsequently thrown open,[3] increased the number of
hands on the sugar plantations. The freedom of
commerce with all the ports of Spain, and occasionally with the neutral powers; the wise administra-

---

[1] The city of Havana surrendered to the British forces, under
Count Albemarle and Admiral Sir George Pocock, on the 12th
August, 1762, after a siege of two months and six days. The
amount of booty divided equally between the army and navy was
£736,185 3s. The English forces also occupied Matanzas and
Mariel, but the greater portion of the island never recognized their
government. It was returned to Spain by the treaty of Paris, and
formally given up on the 6th July, 1763, the English having
remained in possession ten months and twenty-four days. During
this time new life was given to agriculture in Cuba by England's
commercial activity, and by the desire of opening a new mart for
her African slave-traders. (See Pezuela's *Ensayo Historico de la
Isla de Cuba*).

[2] It is stated that in the construction of the Cabañas fortress
alone, fourteen millions of dollars were expended.—H.

[3] By royal decree, of 28th February, 1789.—H.

tion of Don Luis de las Casas; the founding of the
Consulado and the Patriotic Society;[1] the destruction of the French colony of St. Domingo, and the
consequent increase in the value of sugar; the
improvements in machinery and furnaces, due, in
great part, to the refugees from Haiti; the more
intimate intercourse between the planters and the
merchants of Havana; the great amounts of capital
invested in the sugar and coffee plantations; are
causes which have successively influenced the prosperity of Cuba. This has continued to advance,
notwithstanding the evils of conflicting branches of
government, which embarrass the march of progress.[2]

[1] Since suppressed.

[2] The complicated state of the administration of justice and of
jurisdiction is such, that in the "Memoria acerca de la situacion
presente de la Ysla de Cuba," p. 40, twenty-five different civil and
ecclesiastical tribunals are enumerated. These subdivisions of the
administration of justice well explain what we have already stated
regarding the great and increasing number of lawyers.—H.

CHAPTER IX.

AGRICULTURE.

Increase of tithes an evidence of prosperity—Table of agricultural
wealth—Hatos and Potreros (*note*)—Pecuniary relations of planters and merchants—Rate of interest—Slave-trade—Coffee planting
—Product—Yield per hand compared with sugar—[NOTE.—
Decline of coffee planting—Causes.]—Tobacco planting—Former
monopoly—Product—Decline—Factoria — Prices—Quantity purchased, and where sold—Expenses of Factoria—State of tobacco
planting in 1820-5—[NOTE.—Obstacles to tobacco planting—
Future prospects—Present product—Prices—Error of Baron Humboldt—Probable causes of superiority of the tobacco from the
Vuelta de Abajo.]—Other products in Cuba—Wheat—Wine—
Wax.

THE increase of tithes being everywhere one of
the most certain evidences of the increase of public
wealth, I present here a statement of their product
for fifteen years. The tithes and minor ecclesiastical
revenues of the diocess of Havana, were farmed for
terms of four years, as follows:

1789 to 1792	$ 792,386
1793 " 1796	1,044,005
1797 " 1800	1,595,340
1801 " 1804	1,864,464

We see here that the tithes in the last term amounted to the mean annual sum of $466,000, although sugar pays only one-twentieth, or half tithes.[1]

[1] In 1792, coffee, indigo, and cotton were declared exempt from tithes, for ten years; and, in 1804, this exemption was made perpetual, and was extended to sugar plantations then in existence. In 1817, the tithes on sugar were reduced to two and a half per cent. These changes in the law, and the great changes that have occurred since the beginning of the present century in the objects of agricultural labor, have naturally produced a fluctuation in the product of this tax, as many lands that paid tithes, while held as cattle farms, &c., when planted in cane, ceased to contribute, and the product of the impost has been, in a great measure, maintained and increased by the advance of the minor branches of agriculture. It is still farmed out, and is payable in money or kind, being compounded. This tax is most onerous upon the small farmers, upon whom the tithe collectors are very exacting, because of their inability to maintain an expensive litigation, while the large proprietors can always compound on more favorable terms. Sagra states the tithes for the bishopric of Havana, from 1805 to 1828, as follows:

1805 to 1808........$1,545,059	1817 to 1820........$1,606,672
1809 " 1812........ 1,501,212	1821 " 1824........ 1,449,409
1813 " 1816........ 1,600,841	1825 " 1828........ 1,250,805

The tithes of the archbishopric of Cuba also show a diminution. The same writer states them as follows:

1819 to 1822 ....$79,010
1828 " 1826........................ 40,487
1827 " 1830........................ 89,595

The revenue from this tax has recovered, and even surpassed its former yield, being now about $500,000, annually.

The agricultural wealth of the department of Havana, in 1817 was:

Sugar plantations, ...	625	Tobacco plantations,	1,601
Coffee plantations, ...	779	Churches, ...	224
Potreros, ...	1,197	Houses, ...	42,268
¹Haciendas, ...	930		

[NOTE.—That of the three departments is stated as follows, in the census of 1846:

	Sugar Plantations.	Coffee Plantations.	Potreros.	Haciendas.	Tobacco Plantations.	Churches.	Houses.
Western,......	735	1,012	1,548	198	3,990	229	56,104
Central,.......	404	78	4,805	576	967	65	31,079
Eastern, ...	808	580	2,338	470	4,145	86	25,779
Total,......	1,442	1,670	8,691	1,289	9,102	380	112,962

To these, we may add the following number of farms, called *Sitios de labor:* In the Western, 12,286; Central, 6,678; Eastern, 6,328.]

The extraordinary expenditures required by the large sugar plantations, and the frequent domestic

---

¹ The *Hatos* or *Haciendas de Cria*, and the *Potreros*, are cattle farms. The first are often two or three leagues in diameter, without fences, where half-wild cattle are pastured. Two or three horsemen only are necessary on them, who traverse the country looking after the cows, and collecting and marking the calves. The *Potreros* are smaller cattle farms, fenced, and frequently having some land planted in maize, yuca, and plantain. Cattle are there fattened, and sheep, swine, and goats reared.—H.

misfortunes caused by play, luxury, and other evils, place the landed proprietors in a state of absolute dependence upon the merchants. The most frequent loans are those made to the planters, upon condition of repayment from his crop of sugar, or coffee, at prices two rials per arrobe of the first, and two dollars per quintal of the last, less. than the current rates in market. Thus a crop of one thousand boxes of sugar is sold in anticipation, at a loss of $4,000. The demand for money for business transactions, and the scarcity of coin, is so great that the government at times is forced to borrow at ten per cent., and individuals at even twelve and sixteen per cent. interest. The great profits made in the African slave-trade, sometimes amounting on a single voyage in Cuba to 100 or 125 per cent., have contributed to increase the rate of interest; for many parties hire money at 18 or 20 per cent., for the purpose of following this infamous trade. The traffic is not only barbarous in itself, but it is also unreasonable, as it does not attain the object it proposes; for like a stream of water brought from a long distance, more than one-half of it, even in the colonies themselves, is turned aside from the cultivation of the lands for which it was destined.

COFFEE.—The cultivation of coffee, like the improvements in sugar making, dates from the arrival of the immigrants from St. Domingo, or, more particularly, from the years 1796 and 1798. On a coffee plantation having 35,000 trees, a *hectar* of land yields 890 kilogrammes of coffee. In the district of Havana there were, in 1800, 60 coffee plantations, and 779 in 1817. As the coffee tree does not yield abundantly before the fourth year, the export of coffee from the port of Havana, in 1804, was only 50,000 arrobes; since then it has increased. It was in

1809	320,000	1819	642,716
1815	918,263	1820	686,046
1816	370,229	1822	501,429
1817	709,351	1823	895,924
1818	779,618	1824	661,674

These figures show a great variation, which arises from frauds in the custom-house, as well as from more or less abundant crops; for the results of the years 1815, 1816, and 1823, which might be supposed the least exact, have been lately compared with the custom-house returns. We may estimate the total export from Cuba (in 1825) as follows:

From Havana, average from 1814 to 1824	694,000	arrobes.
Matanzas, Trinidad, St. Jago, &c.	220,000	"
Frauds in the custom-house	304,000	"
Total	1,218,000	"

By this calculation it appears that the export of coffee from Cuba is greater than that from Java, which was estimated by Mr. Crawford, in 1820, at 190,000 piculs, or 11¼ kilogrammes; and than that from Jamaica, which, in 1823, did not exceed, according to the custom-house returns, 169,734 cwt., or 8,662.478 kilogrammes.

While the price of sugar in Havana is always quoted by the arrobe, of 25 pounds, that of coffee is quoted by the quintal of 100 pounds. The latter has varied from $3 to $30, and in 1808, it fell even below the former price. During the years 1815–19 it sold from $13 to $17 the quintal, and now rules at $12. It is probable that the cultivation of coffee in Cuba does not employ over 28,000 slaves, the annual average product of which is 305,000 quintals, worth, at present prices, $3,660,000. At the same time, 66,000 negroes produce 440,000 boxes of sugar, which, at the price of $24 a box, are worth $10,560,000. By this estimate we see that each slave produces, annually, in value, $130 in coffee, and $160 in sugar. It is almost needless to observe, that these sums vary with the alterations in price of the two articles named, the variations of which are sometimes in opposite directions, and that in these calculations, which may give some idea of intertropical agriculture, I embrace the domestic consumption, and the licit and contraband export, under the same point of view.

[NOTE.—The product of coffee in Cuba has steadily declined for some years past, under the competition with the greater profits from sugar culture, and the less cost of coffee produced by the cheaper slave labor of Brazil, where, for a series of years before the total cessation of the African slave-trade, in 1851-2, slaves were sold at an average price of $300 to $350. It reached its highest point about 1835, as will be seen by the following tables of exports, compiled from the custom-house returns:

1825 to 1830	Qqs.	2,149,581	Average,	429,716
1830 " 1835	"	2,494,479	"	499,000
1835 " 1840	"	2,347,058	"	469,412
1840 " 1845	"	1,666,247	"	333,249
1845 " 1850	"	960,306	"	192,061
1851	"	143,780		
1852.	"	193,837		

About seventy per cent. of the export in 1852 was from the Eastern department, where the competition of the sugar culture for the employment of slave labor, has not been experienced to the same extent as in the western part of the island.]

TOBACCO.—The tobacco of Cuba is celebrated in

all parts of Europe where smoking prevails; it was introduced there, in imitation of the natives of Haiti, toward the close of the sixteenth, and beginning of the seventeenth century. At one time it was generally believed, that if the cultivation of tobacco was relieved from all the trammels of an odious monopoly, it would be to Havana the source of a great commerce. The beneficent intentions evinced by the government six years since, in abolishing the monopoly of tobacco culture and sale, have not yet produced to this branch of agriculture the benefits which might have been expected. The cultivators are poor, the rent of land has increased in an extraordinary degree, and the preference entertained for coffee planting (in 1825), impedes the increase of the tobacco culture.

The oldest data we possess, relative to the quantity of tobacco supplied by Cuba to the factories of the metropolis, are of the year 1748. According to Raynal, who is a much more exact writer than is generally believed, the yearly average, from 1748 to 1753, was 75,000 arrobes. From 1789 to 1794 the yearly product of the island amounted to 250,000 arrobes; but from that time to 1803, the high price of lands, the preference given to coffee and sugar planting, the vexations arising from the government monopoly of purchase, and the impediments laid upon foreign commerce, have progressively diminished the amount of product to less than one-half that quantity. But it is believed that from 1822 to 1825, the amount of tobacco grown in Cuba has risen to 300,000 or 400,000 arrobes.

The domestic consumption of the island is 200,000 arrobes, or more. Up to the year 1791, the "Commercial Company of Havana ".delivered the tobacco of Cuba to the royal factories in Spain, under contracts which were renewed from time to time with the government. The establishment of a government "Factoria de tabacos" in Havana, succeeded that company, and retained the monopoly of the trade to itself. The tobacco was classified as superior, medium, and inferior, and was received from the growers at fixed prices; in 1804, these were six, five, and two and-a-half dollars per arrobe ($24, $20, and $10 per quintal), respectively. By comparing the different prices with the quantity of each class of tobacco produced, we find that the "Factoria" paid an average price of $16 per quintal for the leaf tobacco. With the expense of manufacture, the segars cost the government seventy-five cents per pound;[1] snuff, fine grain and good color, 42¼ cents,

---

[1] The weight of the segars being about ten pounds to the thousand their cost would be $7 50 per thousand.

and common soft, or Seville, 18¾ cents a pound, in Havana.

In good years, when the crop (the product of advances made by the "Faqtoria" to poor cultivators), amounted to 350,000 arrobes of leaf, 128,000 arrobes were manufactured for Spain, 80,000 for Havana, 9,200 for Peru, 6,000 for Buenos Ayres, 2,240 for Mexico, and 1,100 for Caraccas and Campeachy.[1] In order to make up the amount of 315,000 arrobes (for the crop loses ten per cent. of its weight, in loss and damage in the transportation and manufacture), we must suppose that 80,000 arrobes were consumed in the interior of the island, that is, in the country, where the royal monopoly did not extend.

The maintenance of 120 slaves, and the expenses of manufacture, did not exceed $12,000 yearly; but the salaries of the officers of the "Factoria" amounted to $541,000. The value of the 128,000 arrobes of tobacco sent to Spain, in the abundant years, either in segars, leaf, or snuff, at the customary prices there, exceeded the sum of five millions of dollars.

---

[1] *Situacion actual de la Real Factoria de tabacos de la Habana, en Abril*, 1804.—(Official MSS.). In Seville there were sometimes in store ten or twelve million pounds of tobacco, and the revenue from the tobacco monopoly, in Spain, amounted, in good years, to six millions of dollars.—H.

It is surprising to see in the returns of exports from
Havana (documents published by the *Consulado*),
that the exports for 1816 were only 3,400 arrobes;
for the year 1823, only 13,900 arrobes of leaf tobacco,
and 71,000 pounds of segars, the value of which was
estimated by the custom-house at $281,000; and in
1825, only 70,302 pounds of segars, and 167,100
pounds of leaf tobacco and strips; but we must
remember that no branch of the contraband trade is
more active than that in segars.   The tobacco of the
Vuelta de Abajo is most celebrated, but large quantities are exported which are produced in the eastern
part of the island. Although many travellers state that
the total export of segars in late years, has reached
200,000 boxes (valued at two millions of dollars), I
very much doubt it.   If the crops were so abundant as
this would indicate, why should Cuba receive segars
from the United States for the use of the common
people?

[NOTE.—The cultivation of tobacco has been one
of the most uncertain branches of industry in Cuba.
Trammelled for a long time by odious restrictions
and exactions, it was confined almost entirely to the
poorer classes of the population, who were enabled
to raise a scanty and uncertain crop, through the
advances of capital made them by the "Factoria."

After the suppression of this monopoly, it has had to contend with the more popular and profitable pursuits of coffee and sugar planting, which have successively competed with it for the employment of the skill, capital, and labor of the island. Its increase, however, has been rapid and prosperous, as will be seen by the table of exports below, and with the increasing capital and wealth of Cuba, it is receiving a greater proportion of the labor of the country than has heretofore been bestowed upon it. When a still larger share of the skill and capital now absorbed in the cane-fields, shall be turned to the tobacco *vegas*, we may look for more regular and certain crops, and a corresponding ratio of prosperity. There is also room for great improvement in the classification and method of packing the tobacco.

Export of leaf tobacco and segars from Cuba:

		Tobacco.	Segars.
1825 to 1830.............	Qqs.	128,644	M. 245,097
1830 " 1835.............	"	124,704	" 471,993
1835 " 1840	"	244,259	" 790,285
1840 " 1845.............	"	306,090	" 941,467
1845 " 1850	"	364,183	" 896,008
1851....	"	94,366	" 270,313
1852.............	"	97,374	" 180,610

These figures serve to show the progress of this branch of agriculture, but not its actual state; for

13

the contraband trade in tobacco and segars in Cuba is very great indeed.

During the last twenty years, the prices of segars at Havana have very nearly doubled, and those for leaf tobacco have largely increased. We think Baron Humboldt was misinformed relative to the importation of segars in Cuba, from the United States, for the use of the common people. Some small parcels of manufactured chewing tobacco are imported for sale, and formerly Kentucky tobacco could always be purchased in bond for the African slave-trade; but in our long residence in Cuba, we have never known segars to be imported there from the United States. The *Vuelta de Abajo* owes its fine and universally esteemed quality of tobacco, probably, as much to the physical formation of the country, as to any peculiar quality of its soil. Along the northern border of the district, where the best tobacco is grown, lies the high *Sierra de los Organos*, gathering, in rains upon its northern slopes, the moisture borne landward by the constantly prevailing trade winds; and this, with the effect of the surrounding heated waters of the Caribbean sea, and the Gulf of Mexico, give to the region south of this ridge a character of climate peculiarly its own.]

After speaking of sugar, coffee, and tobacco, the

three products of greatest importance, I will not treat of the cotton, indigo, nor wheat of Cuba. These three branches of colonial industry yield very little, and the proximity of the United States and Guatemala, makes their increase hardly possible. The State of San Salvador exports, at this time, 12,000 bales, or 1,800,000 pounds of indigo, valued at two millions of dollars.

Wheat grows well, to the surprise of travellers who have visited Mexico, in the district of Cuatro Villas, at a slight elevation above the level of the sea; but its cultivation is, in general, very limited. The flour is good, but its production offers few attractions to the colonial agriculturalist; for the fields of the United States, that Crimea of the New World, yield too abundant crops to permit the native cereals to sustain themselves by a system of prohibitive duties, in an island contiguous to the mouths of the Mississippi and Delaware. The same difficulties attend the cultivation of flax, hemp, and the vine.

Even the people of Cuba are not aware, perhaps, that in the first years of the conquest by the Spaniards, wine was made from the juice of wild grapes, in their island. This vine, peculiar to America, has given rise to the very general error that the true *Vitis Vinifera* is common to both continents. The

wild grapes, which gave a slightly acid wine, in
Cuba, were probably gathered from the *Vitis tiliæ-
folia*, which Mr. Wildernow has described in our
herbariums. In no part of the northern hemisphere,
up to this time, has the vine been cultivated for the
purpose of making wine, south of the latitude of
28° 40' which is that of the island of Ferro, one of
the Canaries, and 29° 2', the latitude of Abushcer,
in Persia.

Wax is not produced by indigenous bees (Melipones of Mon. Latreille), but by bees introduced
from Europe by way of Florida. This trade was
not of much importance previous to 1772. The
entire export of the island, from 1774 to 1779, one
year with another, did not exceed 2,700 arrobes;
and, in 1803, it was estimated (including the contraband) at 42,700 arrobes, of which 25,000 went to
Vera Cruz. The churches in Mexico consume largely
of Cuban wax; the price varies from $16 to $20 per
arrobe. The number of arrobes exported from
Havana alone, by the custom-house returns, has
been as follows :

1815	23,398	1820	16,939
1816	22,365	1822	14,450
1817	20,076	1823	15,692
1818	24,156	1824	16,058
1819	19,373	1825	16,505

[NOTE.—From all the island—

1840 to 1845	187,035	1851	57,453
1845 " 1850	290,000	1852	58,591]

Trinidad, and the small port of Baracoa, have also a considerable trade in wax, which is gathered in the uncleared portions of the country. The vicinity of the sugar plantations destroys many bees, for they become drunken with the refuse of the sugar kettles and the molasses, of which they are very fond. In general, the production of wax declines as the lands are brought under cultivation.

CHAPTER X.

COMMERCE.

Causes of its importance—Wealth of Cuba—Relation of Havana to
Spanish-America—Present state of commerce—Official valuations
(*Note*)—Fallacies of tables of trade—Remarks thereon—
Balanza de Comercio—Imports and exports, 1816 and 1823—
Character of imports—Of exports—Merchant ships and men-of-
war at Havana—[NOTE.—Imports and exports, 1852—Character
of imports, and proportion from United States—Exports—Proportion to the United States—Vessels entered and cleared—Proportion of commerce of Havana.]—Reflections on the character of
importations—Large amount of woven fabrics—Of provisions and
liquors—State of society, and want of subsistence—Mines and
cereals a necessity—Surprising importation of meats and pulse—
Probable future deduced—Error of the deduction (*Note*)—Evil
colonial policy of Europe—Not adapted to Cuba—Probable
increase of population—Social theory—Law of public welfare
and of future of Cuba—[NOTE.—Error of social theory demonstrated by Jamaica—Transition of blacks from slavery to freedom
—Its sad results—Tendency of free negroes to abandon the fields
—Natural results—Sustains Baron Humboldt's law of public
welfare and of future of Cuba.]—Flour trade—Mexican competition—State of public wealth in 1800—Its increase—Cuban defence
of free trade—Influence of commerce upon society—Progress not
to be measured by *tons*—Lives of nations.

IT has been already stated, in the beginning of
this work, that the importance of the commerce of

Cuba does not arise solely from the wealth of its products, nor from its demand for the wares and fabrics of Europe; but that this importance is based, in part, upon the admirable situation of the port of Havana, at the entrance of the Mexican Gulf, and immediately where the great routes of the commercial nations of both worlds cross each other. The Abbé Raynal has said, at a time when its agriculture contributed, in sugar and coffee, barely two millions to the commerce of the world, "The island of Cuba alone may be worth a kingdom to Spain."

These memorable words have been, in some degree, prophetic, and since she has lost Mexico, Peru, and so many other States that have attained their independence, they should be seriously pondered by the statesmen who may guide the political interests of Spain. The island of Cuba, to which the court of Madrid has long since conceded great freedom of trade, exports, through licit and illicit channels, its own productions of sugar, coffee, tobacco, wax, and hides, to the amount of fourteen millions of dollars at the present time (1825). This is only one-third less than that of Mexico at the time of her greatest mining prosperity. It may be said, that Havana and Vera Cruz are to the rest of America, what New York is to the United States. The tonnage of the thousand or twelve hundred merchant ships that annually arrive at the port of

Havana, amounts (exclusive of the smaller craft engaged in the coasting trade) to 150,000 or 170,000 tons. We also see, even in a time of peace, from 120 to 150 vessels of war touching annually at that port.

From 1815 to 1819 the value of the products registered at the custom-house of Havana alone (sugar, rum, molasses, coffee, wax, and hides), amounted to $11,245,000, one year with another. In 1823, the value of her exports, returned at less than two-thirds of their actual prices (and exclusive of $1,179,000 in coin), has exceeded the sum of $12,500,000. It is more than probable that the imports of the whole island, licit and contraband, estimated at the actual value of the goods and the slaves, amount, at the present time, to fifteen or sixteen millions of dollars, of which barely three or four millions are re-exported.[1] Havana purchases

---

[1] The official returns of the value of exports and imports in Cuba, in 1851 and 1852, are as follows:

	Imports.	Exports.	Exports to Enid.
1851	$34,042,740	$33,654,888	$1,718,085
1852	30,928,711	28,602,912	1,148,975

In these returns the rates of valuation for exports are, for sugar 3½ cents per pound; molasses $6¼ a hhd, (about 5 cents a gallon); rum 16 cents a gallon; coffee 4 cents a pound; segars $4 ʌ thousand; leaf tobacco 6 and 12½ cents a pound; copper ore $2 50 per quintal.

in foreign marts much larger quantities of goods
than are needed for her own consumption, exchanging her colonial products for the fabrics of Europe,
and selling them again at Vera Cruz, Truxillo,
Laguaira, and Carthagena.

I have examined in another work, fifteen years
since, the basis upon which are founded the tables
published "under the fallacious title of *Balanzas de
Comercio;*" and I stated then how little confidence
can be reposed in these pretended accounts between
nations making mutual exchanges, the advantages of
which it is believed can only be appreciated, under
a false principle of political economy, by the amount
of balances paid in coin. The following statistics
will exhibit two years from the *Balanzas* and *Esta-
dos de Comercio,* arranged by order of the government. I have altered none of the figures, for they
present (and this is a great advantage in treating of
quantities which are difficult to estimate) the minimum amounts.

The values stated in these tables, are neither the
actual values of the articles at the place of production, nor those of the markets of sale; but they
are fictitious valuations, *official values,* as they are
termed in the custom-house system of Great Britain,
that is to say (and I shall never tire of repeating it),
one-third less than the current prices. In order to

ascertain, with the tables of the trade of Havana as
given by the Spanish custom-houses, the commerce
of the whole island, we should require tables of the
returns of imports and exports from all the other
ports, and add to the sum total the amount of fraudu-
lent trade, which varies with different places, and
to know the nature of goods and the changes in their
prices from year to year. Such estimates can only
be made by the local authorities; and the matter
that has been published by these, in the struggle
with the Spanish Cortes which they have maintained with so much ability, proves that they do
not deem themselves sufficiently prepared for a labor
which embraces so many objects at the same time.

The *Junta de Gobierno* and the *Real Consulado*
publish annually, under the title of *Balanza de Comercio*, tables of the custom-house returns of exports
and imports through the port of Havana alone;[1] in
which a distinction is drawn between the imports in
Spanish and foreign vessels, the exports for Spain, for
Spanish ports in America, and for ports not under
the dominion of the Spanish crown. The weight or
measure of the merchandise, its official value, and
the royal and municipal duties are also expressed;

[1] Although I possess a large number of these, I only publish in
this work the figures which are absolutely necessary to guide us to
general results.—H.

but the official estimates of the prices of goods, as
we have before stated, are much below their market
value.[1]

IMPORTS.

	1816.	1822.
In Spanish vessels—		
Fabrics and merchandise,...$1,032,135		
African slaves, ... 2,659,950		No slaves
Gold and silver,........... 2,288,358		reported.
	5,980,443	$ 3,562,227
In foreign vessels,........... 7,239,543		10,136,538
Total,...................$13,219,968		$13,968,735

EXPORTS.

In Spanish vessels—		
For Spain, ...$2,419,424		
Spanish ports in America, .. 2,104,890		
Coast of Africa,........... 643,852		
	5,267,966	$3,550,312
Foreign vessels,........... 3,195,169		8,778,857
Total,...............$8,363,135		$12,329,169

[1] For example, each negro is valued at $150, and each barrel of
flour at $10. After expressing the total amounts of fallacious
balanzas de comercio, I have indicated the sums of gold and silver
which have passed through Cuba. In order to give an approximate
idea of the domestic consumption of the island, and its requirements
of European manufactures, I have stated the quantity of the same
articles imported and re-exported.—H.

The custom-house returns of gold and silver exported in 1816, amount to $480,840, and in 1823, to $1,179,034 imported, and $1,404,584 exported. Among the imports and exports, we find the following articles:

	1816.		1823.	
	Imported.	Re-exported.	Imported.	Re-exported.
Flour (bbls.),................	71,907	10,965	74,119	—
Wines and liquors from Europe, $	468,067	111,466	1,119,487	49,286
Salt meats and provisions,....	1,096,791	237,274	—	—
Manufactured clothing, ...	127,681	4,695	213,226	—
Linen goods, ...	3,226,859	1,529,610	2,071,063	29,596
Woolen　"　................	103,324	—		
Cotton　"　..............	—	—	1,021,807	69,049
Furniture, glass ware, &c.,....	267,312	29,000	464,326	8,046
Paper,......................	61,846	20,496	156,837	22,268
Iron ware,..................	330,368	99,581	288,697	68,149
Hides and skins,.............	135,108	—	—	—
Lumber and wooden ware,....	285,217	—	858,766	29,452
Rice (lbs.),.................	—	—	7,746,025	—
Lard (kegs), ...	—	—	89,948	—
Jerked beef (lbs.),..........	—	—	10,786,600	—

The products of the island exported were as folllows.

			1816.	1823.
Sugar, ...	Boxes,		200,481	300,211
Coffee, ...	Arrobes,		370,229	895,925
Wax, ...	"		22,365	15,962
Molasses,...........	Hhds.		—	30,145
Leaf tobacco,.......	Arrobes,		—	13,879
Segars,....	Pounds,		—	71,108

The most exact data I have been able to obtain, relative to the arrivals and departures of vessels at the port of Havana, are the following:

Arrivals, 1799	883	1802	845
1800	784	1803	1,020
1801	1,015		

Average from 1815 to 1819, ... 1,192

	Merchant vessels.		Men-of-war.
	Arrived.	Sailed.	Arrived.
1820	1,305	1,230	—
1821	1,268	1,168	95
1822	1,182	1,118	141
1823	1,168	1,144	149
1824	1,086	1,088	129

[NOTE.—In order that the reader may see, at a glance, the progress and present state of the commerce of Cuba, we insert here the results exhibited in the *Balanza de Comercio* of 1852.

IMPORTS.

In 947 Spanish vessels,	$20,325,751
2,665 Foreign "	9,454,491
3,612	$29,780,242

EXPORTS.

In 819 Spanish vessels	$ 7,018,018
" 2,455 Foreign "	20,435,919
3,274	27,453,937

Imports in bond	$1,048,469
Exports " "	1,148,975

The importations for domestic consumption are lassed as follows:—

	Total.	From U. States.
Cotton Goods	$2,661,568	$144,552
Linen "	2,431,564	75,580
Woolen "	359,060	15,663
Silk "	598,747	64,193
Manufactures of Leather	635,374	38,663
Meats	1,909,394	161,950
Fish	668,425	152,171
Wines and Liquors	2,563,303	64,433
Flour	4,084,286	91,714
Rice	1,046,604	811,462
Grain and Pulse	320,212	115,991
Spices and Fruits	397,439	22,469
Other Provisions	1,400,005	287,900
Lard and Butter	948,144	902,635
Lumber	2,042,187	1,864,997
Metals and Iron ware	2,476,106	201,469
Soap	581,068	64,624
Other Manufactures	3,936,274	958,200
Live Stock	40,206	9,157
Material for Railroads and Sugar Mills	680,276	269,223
Specie	989,424	532,468
	$29,780,242	$6,849,514

EXPORTS.

	Total.	To U. States.
Sugar	$20,153,002	$8,940,050
Molasses	1,603,929	978,687
Rum	229,437	11,580
Carry forward	$21,986,368	$9,930,317

	Total.	To U. States.
Brought forward	$21,986,368	$9,930,317
Coffee	739,369	138,901
Segars	764,414	353,945
Leaf Tobacco....	1,001,166	274,316
Copper Ore	945,532	39,080
Other Products..	2,017,088	1,339,850
	$27,453,937	$12,076,409

The United States supplied 23 per cent. of the imports, and received 47 per cent. of the exports. The exportation of the principal staples is thus stated :—

		Total.	To U. States.		
Sugar.... ....Boxes		1,409,012	638,578 or 44 per cent.		
Molasses ....Hhds.		262,593	156,590 " 61 "		
Rum............Pipes		11,359	579 " 5 "		
Coffee ....Arrobes		739,369	138,901 " 19 · "		
Segars ....M.		180,610	84,887 " 46 "		
Leaf Tobacco.....Qqls.		97,374	27,711 " 27 "		
Copper Ore....... "		381,470	15,632 " 4 "		

Of the 3,612 vessels entered, 1,886 were American, and of the 3,274 cleared, 1,644 were American. Tonnage entered 622,016 tons.

Of the imports 74 per cent., and of the exports 44 per cent. were through the port of Havana.]

When we compare in these tables the great value of the importations with the small value of the goods re-exported, we are surprised to find how great is the domestic consumption of a country, containing only 325,000 white, and 130,000 free colored population. Estimating the several articles at their current prices, we find a consumption of two and a half or three millions of dollars in linen goods, one million in cotton goods, four hundred thousand in silks, and two hundred and twenty thousand in woolen goods. The demand of Cuba, through the port of Havana alone, for the woven fabrics of Europe, has exceeded four, or four and a half millions of dollars yearly, for the last few years. To these imports at Havana, through licit channels, we must add for furniture, glass ware, &c., &c. $500,000; iron and steel, $380,000; lumber, $400,000; and castile soap, $300,000.

The importations of provisions and liquors at Havana, seem to me, worthy the attention of those who wish to ascertain the true social state of those communities called the *sugar colonies*. Such is the composition of society in those communities, inhabiting the most fertile soil that Nature has offered to the use of man; such the direction of agricultural labor and industry in the Antilles, that in the beneficent climate of the tropics the people would fail to obtain subsistence, if it were not for the freedom and activity of their foreign commerce.

I will not refer to the wines imported at Havana, which amounted (according to the custom-house returns, be it remembered) to 40,000 barrels in 1803, and in 1823 to 15,000 pipes, valued at $1,200,000; nor to the 6,000 barrels of brandies, &c., from Spain and Holland; nor to the 113,000 barrels of flour. These wines, these liquors, and this flour, to the value of $3,300,000, are consumed only by the better classes of the people. The cereals of the United States have become a real and true necessity, under a zone where for a long time, maize, yuca, and the plantain were preferred to any other kind of food. Amid the always-increasing enlightenment of Havana, we may not lament the development of a luxury that is purely European. But alongside of the flour, wines, and liquors of Europe we find, in 1816, a million, and in 1823, three and a half millions of dollars in *salted meats, rice*, and *dried pulse*. During the last named year, the importation of rice (in Havana alone, and by the custom-house returns, exclusive of contraband), has been 8,075,000 pounds (in 1852, in all the island, 20,940,925 pounds), that of salted and dried meats, the *tasajo* (jerked beef), so necessary for the support of the slaves, 11,625,000 pounds (in all the island, in 1852, 41,750,450 pounds).

This absence of the means of subsistence characterizes that part of the tropical regions where the unwise activity of the European has inverted the order of nature. It will diminish as the inhabitants become better aware of their true interests, and disheartened at the low prices of colonial products, and they will then vary the staples of their production, and give an impulse to all the branches of rural economy.[1]

The principles of the limited and mean policy which guides the rulers of small islands (workshops, in fact, dependent upon Europe, and inhabited by men who abandon the country as soon as they become sufficiently wealthy), can never harmonize with a country nearly as large in extent as England, filled with populous cities, and whose inhabitants, descending from father to son for centuries, far from deeming themselves strangers upon American soil, hold for it the same affection that every one entertains for his native land.

[1] The study and development of the true principles of Political Economy, during the last quarter of a century, have demonstrated the reverse of this theory of material interests. It is now generally admitted that the labor and capital of a country are most wisely employed in the production of those staples for which its climate and soil are best adapted. In this manner, through the interchanges of a free trade, the wants of the community are supplied with the least expenditure of labor, and a larger portion of its produced wealth is left in the form of capital, to be re-applied to production. It is this combination of agriculture and commerce that has been the source of the great material prosperity of Cuba.

The population of the island of Cuba, which perhaps, may increase within fifty years to a million, may open to itself, through its own wants, an immense field to native industry.

Though the slave-trade should cease, and the slaves pass slowly to the condition of freemen, and society attain the power of self-government, without being exposed to the violent fluctuations of civil commotion, it would continue upon the path marked out by nature for every numerous and intelligent community. The cultivation of sugar and coffee would not, therefore, be abandoned, but like that of cochineal in Mexico, of indigo in Guatemala, and of cocoa in Venezuela, it would cease to be the principal basis of national existence. An intelligent and free agricultural people would succeed a slave population that is without foresight or industry. The capital which the commerce of Havana has poured into the hands of the agriculturists during the last fifteen years, is already beginning to change the face of the country, and to this efficient power, whose action is always increasing, there would necessarily be added another—the development of human knowledge, which is inseparable from the progress of industry and of national wealth. On the union of these two great springs of action depends the future fate of the metropolis of the Antilles.

[NOTE.—The error of the social theory here stated
has been demonstrated by the sad experience of
Jamaica. The change in the condition of the blacks
in that island was made in accordance with the
requisites here laid down, as far as it was possible to
accord with them. The transition of the slaves to
the condition of freemen was gradual, and the amal-
gamated community attained the right of self-government without the violent fluctuations of civil commotion ; yet it has been found that an intelligent and
free agricultural people did not succeed the slave
population; that the numbers and influence of the
intelligent white population have steadily and
rapidly decreased, and threaten to become wholly
extinct; that the freed negroes are relapsing from
the semi-intelligent state they had attained under the
rule of the whites, and are retrograding toward barbarism; that the supply of agricultural labor, and
consequently, the product of agriculture, has largely
diminished; that commerce has dwindled away;
and that the social condition of the blacks has sunk
to an unhappy prevalence of sloth, misery, and
want.

Co-existent with this decline in the material
welfare of the inhabitants of Jamaica, a decline in
their moral condition has been experienced. Religion
has waned; churches have been closed; schools

have fallen into decay; the ministers of the gospel have fled the country; the rite of marriage is falling into disuse; the social position of woman has been degraded; and vice and crime have become, in a measure, natural to the state of society among the mass of negroes. The statistics of population in Cuba, which we have already examined, demonstrate the same tendency of the free blacks there to abandon the labors of agriculture, and to congregate in the towns. The cultivation of the fields being thus diminished, commerce, which is the handmaiden of agriculture, must decline also, and with this diminution ceases the accession of capital, which commerce brings to the agriculturist.

In these sad facts, we recognize the truth of the social law laid down by Baron Humboldt: that "the development of human knowledge is inseparable from the progress of industry and of national wealth;" and we must also admit his deduction, that the future fate of Cuba depends upon the maintenance of her industry, and the increase of her national wealth, which shall continue to extend the magic influence of capital over her fields, and stimulate the development of knowledge among the people.]

The custom-house returns of flour imported at

Havana alone, in 1823, was 113,506 barrels, which, at the average price of $16 50, inclusive of the duties, amounts to $1,864,500. The first direct importation of flour from the United States is due to the wise administration of Don Luis de las Casas. Before his time, it could only be imported after having been carried to a port in Europe. Mr. Robinson (*Mem. on the Mexican Revolution*, vol. 2, p. 380) estimates the importation of flour into Cuba, through licit and illicit channels, at 120,000 barrels. He adds, which seems to me less certain, "that the island of Cuba, in consequence of the evil distribution of slave labor there, could barely sustain a blockade of five months." In 1822, there were imported from the United States 144,980 barrels, valued in Havana, inclusive of the duties, at $2,391,000.

[In 1852, the total importation of flour into Cuba was 327,950 barrels, of which but 7,610 were from the United States; total value, at the mean selling price of $16 50, $5,411,175.]

Notwithstanding that the flour of the United States is burdened with an impost of seven dollars a barrel, yet that of Spain—Santander, for instance

—cannot compete with it.[1] A competition was begun by Mexico, under the most favorable circumstances; for, during my residence at Vera Cruz, Mexican flour was already exported from there to the value of three hundred thousand dollars; and this had increased, in 1809, to 70,000 barrels, as is shown by the statement of Mr. Pitkins. The political disturbances of Mexico have entirely destroyed this trade in cereals, between two countries both situate under the torrid zone, but at different elevations above the level of the sea, which exerts a powerful influence upon climate and production.

As a complement to these statements regarding the foreign trade of Cuba, let us listen to the author of an essay we have repeatedly cited, who sets forth the true situation of the island. " Havana begins already to experience the effects of an accumulation of wealth, for provisions have doubled in price, within a few years, and the wages of labor are so increased, that a newly imported African, without having learned any trade, earns by the labor of his hands from 50 to 62½ cents a day; and a negro mechanic, however rough his work, earns from 62½ to

---

[1] The duty on flour imported from the United States is now nearly eleven dollars a barrel, and is an efficient protection to that of Santander.

75 cents a day. The patrician families remain in the country, and those who become rich do not return to Europe. There are families which are very wealthy: Don Mateo Pedroso, who died a short time since, left in land alone more than two millions of dollars. The trade which is transacted yearly in that market amounts to more than twenty millions."—*De la situacion presente de Cuba.*—*MSS.*

Such was the state of public wealth at the close of the year 1800. Since then, twenty-five years of constantly increasing prosperity have elapsed, and the population has nearly doubled. Previous to 1800, the returns of the export of sugar did not reach 170,000 boxes; now (1825) it always exceeds 200,000 boxes, and has attained 250,000, and even 300,000. [In 1852, it exceeded 1,400,000 boxes.] A new branch of industry has been created in the coffee culture, the export of which shows a value of three and a half millions of dollars. Industry, directed by better knowledge, has attained better results, and the system of imposts that bore heavily upon it, and weighed down foreign trade, was changed in the year 1791, and has been subsequently improved by successive alterations.

Whenever the mother country, ignoring her true interests, has wished to take a retrograde step, a thousand clamors, each louder than the other, have come up, not only from the people of Havana, but frequently also from Spanish executive officers, in defence of the freedom of trade in America. Through the enlightened zeal and patriotic views of the intendant, Don Claudio Martinez Pinillos, another step has been recently taken, favoring the employment of capital, in conceding to Havana a warehousing system or trade in bond, under the most favorable auspices.

In Havana, as everywhere, where commerce and its consequent wealth experience a rapid increase, the evil influence it exercises over ancient customs is complained of. This is not the place to compare the former state of Cuba, covered with pasture before its capture by the English, and its present state, when it has become the metropolis of the Antilles; neither will we weigh the frankness and simplicity of the customs of a nascent society, with those which appertain to a more advanced civilization. A love of wealth springs from the spirit of commerce, and as a necessary consequence, the mass contemns whatever cannot be obtained with money; but it is the good fortune of human affairs, that whatever is most worthy of being desired, most noble and most free in man, we owe only to the inspirations of the soul, and to the improvement of our intellectual faculties.

14

If the pursuit of wealth should pervade to an
absolute degree all classes of society, it would infal-
libly produce the evil that is deplored by those who
contemplate with sorrow what they style the preponderance of the industrial system.   But the increase
of commerce—multiplying the friendly ties between
nations, opening an immense sphere to the operations of the mind, pouring capital into the lap of
agriculture, and creating new wants through the
refinements of luxury—presents in itself the remedy
for the danger which they believe to exist.   In this
extreme complication of cause and effect, time is
needed to establish the equilibrium between the different classes of society.   We cannot say, at any
given period, that civilization, the progress of knowledge, and the development of the public mind,
may be measured by *tons*, by the value of exports,
or by the state of the industrial arts.   Nations, like
individuals, should not be judged by a single period
of their lives, for they must run the entire course of
their destiny, passing through the whole scale of a
civilization adequate to their physical condition, and
consonant with their national character.

CHAPTER XI.

INTERNAL COMMUNICATIONS.

Projected canal from Havana to Batabanó—Survey and levels—
Difficulty of making roads—Estimated cost and advantages of the
Canal—[NOTE.—Present state of roads—Itinerary of principal
roads—Cross-roads—Turnpikes—Introduction of railroads—Their
adaptability to Cuba—Government determines to build the first—
Its immense cost—Receipts and expenses—Sale and extension—
Present system of railroads—Existing railroads in Cuba—Their
cost—Receipts—Steam navigation—Coasting trade—Shipbuilding
—Telegraph.]

THE laborious and costly means of internal communication in Cuba, increase the cost of her
products in her ports, notwithstanding the short
distance between the northern and southern shore.
A projected canal, which shall combine the advantages of uniting Havana with Batabanó, and diminish, at the same time, the expense of transportation
to the native products, is worthy of special mention
here. The idea of the Güines canal was conceived
more than half a century since, for the single purpose of supplying the Navy-yard of Havana with

ship timber at a moderate price. In 1796 Count
Jaruco y Mopox, an estimable and enterprising gentleman, who possessed great influence at court
through his intimacy with the Prince of the Peace,
undertook the revival of this project, and in 1798
the survey was made by two engineers of great
merit,[1] Don Francisco and Don Felix Lemaur, who
found that the length of the canal would be nineteen
leagues, of five thousand varas each; that the highest point was at the Taverna del Rey, and that
nineteen locks on the northern slope, and twenty-one
on the southern, would be required. In a direct
line there are only eight and one-third maritime
leagues, from Havana to Batabanó. The canal of
Güines, even as a canal for the smaller navigation,
would be of great utility in the transportation of
agricultural products by steam vessels, for it would
pass through the most highly cultivated lands.

In no part of the world do the roads become more
impassable during the rainy season, than in that part
of the island, where the soil is a decomposing limestone ill adapted to the making of wheel-roads.
The transportation of sugar from Güines to Havana,

---

[1] This survey gave the following elevations in Burgos feet;
Cerro, near the bridge of the Zanja, 106.2; Taverna del Rey,
329.3; town of Rincon, 295.3; lagoon of Zaldivar, when filled up,
237.3; Quivican, 166.1; Village of Batabanó, 21.3.—H.

a distance of twelve leagues, costs now one dollar a quintal. Besides the advantages that would accrue to the internal communications, the canal would give great importance to the roadstead of Batabanó, which could be available to small vessels laden with jerked beef from Venezuela, which would thus avoid doubling Cape San Antonio. In the stormy season, and in time of war, when privateers are cruising between Cape Catoche, the Tortugas, and Mariel, it would be advantageous to shorten the voyage from the Spanish main to Cuba, by arriving, not at Havana, but at some port on the south side of island.

In 1796 the probable cost of the Güines canal was estimated at a million, or one million two hundred thousand dollars; we may suppose it would now cost a million and a half of dollars. The products that might pass annually through the canal have been estimated at 75,000 boxes of sugar, 25,000 arrobes of coffee, and 8,000 hhds. of molasses and rum. In the first project, that of 1796, it was intended to connect the canal with the Güines brook, running it from the Holanda sugar estate towards Quivican, three leagues south of Bejucal and Santa Rosa. This idea has now been abandoned, as the Güines brook loses its water toward the east, in the irrigation of the savannas of Guana-

mon. Instead of leading the canal east of the
Cerro village, and south of the castle of Atares to
the bay itself, the intention was to avail of the bed
of the Chorrera or Almendares river, from Calaba-
zal to Husillo, and thence to follow the royal zanja;
thus bringing the vessels into the suburbs and city of
Havana, and at the same time, supplying the fountains with water, of which they are now deprived
during three months of the year. I have had the
pleasure of visiting, in company with Messieurs
Lemaur, the country through which this line of navigation should pass. The utility of the project is
undeniable, if, in a time of great drought, a sufficient supply of water can be brought to the dividing point.

[NOTE.—The projected canal was never constructed, but the facilities for internal communication in Cuba have largely increased since the time
of Baron Humboldt's writing, and a short sketch of
their present condition will not be inappropriate in
a view of the actual condition of the island. The
old system of highways, which is still in use, is a
series of roads upon which very little labor has
been expended, and during the rainy season travelling on them is exceedingly laborious. The principal road running east from Havana, is the great

highway through the island, and the mail is still carried over it on horseback. Its principal points are, to Matanzas, 21 leagues; thence to Villa Clara, 57 l.; to Santi Espiritu, 23 l.; to Puerto Principe, 50 l.; to Las Tunas, 31 l.; to Bayamo, 14 l.; to St. Jago de Cuba, 34 l.; to Santa Catalina, 25 l.; to Baracoa, 44 l.; total, 299 leagues. Two roads run west from Havana (the Central and the South Shore roads), to Pinar del Rio, 45 l.; and thence to Guane, 15 l.; and to Mantua, 6 leagues. Total, 66 leagues. Another road runs west from Havana, along the northern shore, to Mariel, 14 leagues; thence to Cabañas, 5 l.; to Bahia Honda, 6 l.; and thence to Mantua. The southern road runs from Havana to Güines, 12 leagues; thence to Cienfuegos, 57 l.; and to Trinidad, 21 l.; total, 90 leagues.

There are also, a common road along the northern side, highways across the island in several places, as from Matanzas to Cienfuegos; from Sagua to Cienfuegos, through Villa Clara; Remedios to Trinidad, through Villa Clara; Moron to Santi Espiritu and Saza; Nuevitas, through Puerto Principe, to Santa Cruz; Gibara to Holguin, Bayamo, and Manzanillo: and others between the larger towns. Besides these principal roads, there are numerous cross country roads, and innumerable paths, used by the country people. Of all these roads, we may

observe generally, that in the Western department
they are fair, in the Central poor, and in the
Eastern impracticable for wheel-carriages. The
common roads are little more than open portions of
country, left for public transit, and being without
grading or repair of any kind upon them, partake of
the qualities of the land where they may be located.
In places hilly, stony, and dangerous, in others, they
have a deep alluvial soil, intransitable except in the
dry season. Travelling is, therefore, a matter of no
little trouble and delay, and the consequent small
number of travellers enables Cuba to dispense with
those, in other countries, necessary institutions,
hotels and taverns; and their absence has given rise
to that generous country hospitality so often noted by
tourists in Cuba.

Many years since, a turnpike system was devised,
to extend over the most populous portions of the
island, but the great labor and expense of constructing roads sufficiently stable to resist the heavy rains
of the tropics, made the progress of these very slow.
A few short ones have been constructed in the
vicinity of Havana, and are still being extended.
The principal turnpike runs west from Havana 12
leagues to Guanajay. The southern turnpike extends
to Santiago de las Vegas 5 leagues; the southeastern
is finished for a distance of 7½ leagues, and the

eastern, 5 leagues from Havana. They are constructed by the *Junta de Fomento*, with funds appropriated mostly by the government from the general revenue.

To Don Eduardo Fesser, a private gentleman of Havana, belongs the honor of having first drawn public attention in Cuba to the railroads for internal communication. With unwearied exertion he procured and presented, in a well-digested form, the fullest and most satisfactory information on the subject, and succeeded in establishing a joint stock company for the purpose of carrying his plans into execution. Experience has fully demonstrated the great adaptability of this system of internal communication to the wants of Cuba. The difficulty and great expense of building and keeping in repair good common roads, under the intertropical torrent rains, and the facilities afforded by the face of the country for building railroads without deep cuts, tunnels, or heavy grades, makes their cost comparatively small, while the practicability of constructing short stretches inland, from the harbors, and their becoming immediately profitable, has been favorable to their extension. The wealth and production of the Western department are now in a great measure concentrated upon Havana by a well-devised system of railroads.

14*

At the eleventh hour, the Spanish authorities determined to reserve to themselves the honor of building the first railroad, and M. Fesser and his company were set aside. A loan of two and-a-half millions of dollars was obtained in England, the *Junta de Fomento* contributed $40,000 annually from its funds, the government loaned *emancipados* and convicts as laborers, and the road from Havana to Güines was built. It was commenced in 1835, and opened to Bejucal, 17 miles, in November 1837, and finally to Güines, 44½ miles, in December 1839.

The building of this road is an instructive example of the manner in which public works are carried on by the Spanish authorities in Cuba. Don Pio Pita Pizarro, who was finance minister in Spain in 1839, states in his work on the treasury and national debt of that country, published in Madrid in 1840, that the total cost of the Güines road was $3,909,625 75, being $87,366 per mile, for a single track, and including the cost of equipment, stations, &c., about $95,000 a mile. The government retained the road for three years, during which its receipts were as follows :—

	Passengers.	Freight.	Total.
1839	$171,791	$136,484	$308,275
1840	172,611	173,509	346,120
1841	168,167	181,963	350,140

The expenditures have not been published, but Señor Pizarro, in the work above referred to, states that it required an annual outlay of $441,561 to meet the expenses of the road. The government accordingly determined to sell it, and in 1842 transferred it to a private company that assumed the loan, and engaged to extend the lines. This they have since done to Union, 33½ miles further, where it meets the Matanzas road, and have also constructed branches to Guanajay, 21 miles, and Batabanó, 10 miles.

This road, which is the great trunk of the railway system in Cuba, runs from Havana in a south direction to San Felipe, 26 miles, where it bends to the east through Güines to Union. At Rincon, 14 miles from Havana, the Guanajay branch commences running westward to San Antonio, where it turns toward the north, and at Guanajay it is only six miles from Mariel, on the northern shore of the island. The Matanzas road has a general south course to Union, where it turns to the east, extending through Navajas to Isabel, 25 miles further. The Cardenas road runs south to Bemba, 18 miles, where it bends to the southwest, extending to Navajas, 11 miles—connecting there with the Matanzas road. It has a branch from Bemba, running southeast to Agüica, 33½ miles, which it is contemplated to extend eastward, through the centre of the island, to Villa Clara. The Cienfuegos road runs northward to Cruces, 18 miles, and is being extended to Villa Clara, 18 miles further, where it will connect with the Cardenas road, and through it with the Havana system. The Coliseo road runs eastward from Matanzas to within a few leagues of Cardenas. The Jucaro road runs southeast from Cardenas into what is now the richest sugar district of Cuba. Several other roads are in contemplation, in order to extend the connections of this system both east and west.

The following are the existing roads in Cuba, with their length in English miles:

Havana, with two branches, ...	108¼
Regla to Guanabacoa, ...	2¼
Matanzas, ...	47
Coliseo, ...	24
Cardenas, with one branch, ...	62¼
Jucaro, with one branch, ...	34
Cienfuegos, ...	18
Remedios, ...	6
Trinidad to Casilda, ...	3
Puerto Prinçipe to Nuevitas, ...	46
Cobre to St. Jago, ...	9
Total, ...	360¼

We have stated the cost of the road built by the

government, but that is no criterion for the cost of railroads in Cuba—those built by private enterprise having been equally well constructed, at a much less expense. The road from Cardenas to Navajas cost something less than $28,000 per mile, and the Jucaro road about $20,000 per mile, exclusive of running equipment.[1]

The receipts of the principal of these roads, according to the latest data in our possession, is as follows:

Road.	Length.	1850.		1851.	
		Passengers.	Freight.	Passengers.	Freight.
Havana, ..	108¼	$293,300	$377,209	$336,076	$454,961
Matanzas, .	47	75,876	228,266	87,239	288,782
Coliseo, ...	24	16,691	105,659	13,333	128,526
Cardenas, .	62¼	32,070	158,374	61,695	258,378
Jucaro, ...	34	14,088	291,641	9,103	261,544
Remedios,.	6 (opened April, 1851),......			16,905	22,877

Several lines of steamers are established, con-

[1] For much of this information regarding the railroads of Cuba, we are indebted to a lucid manuscript report drawn up several years since, by C. D. Tolme, Esq., formerly British consul, and still a resident at Havana, whose varied and accurate information relative to Cuba is probably unsurpassed by that of any foreigner there. We have also to acknowledge our obligations to the modest but valuable work of Don José G. de Arboleya, entitled "Manual de la Ysla de Cuba."

necting all the principal ports with Havana, and an
active trade is carried on by them. The lines on the
south coast connect with the Havana railroad, at
Batabanó. In summer from six to eight, and in
winter from ten to twelve steamers, are kept constantly running.

Neither the "Balanzas de Comercio" nor the
"Cuadro Estadistico" give us any information in
relation to the coastwise trade by sea, although it is
very large, the entries at the Havana custom-house
in 1851, of vessels employed in this trade having
amounted to 3,493. The returns of the marine
department show that 433 vessels of twenty tons
burden and upwards, and 1,289 under twenty tons,
are matriculated, three-fourths of which are supposed to be engaged in the domestic coasting trade.
This is by no means improbable, as the number of
vessels employed in this trade is very great, the
general movement of freight upon the railroads
being to the nearest seaport, whence it is conveyed
by sea to Havana. The larger class are generally
schooners, constructed on the finest models, and
many of them are built in Cuba from the admirable
timber furnished by her forests—mahogany being
often used in the frame, and cedar in planking
them. Within a short time steam propellers have

been advantageously introduced in this trade, for which they seem eminently adapted. The electric telegraph has lately been introduced, but being entirely in the hands of the government it is of little service to the public.

CHAPTER XII.

REVENUE.

Historical sketch—Its comparatively large amount—Causes of great
expenditure—Struggle with the Spanish republics—Mistaken
policy of Spain—Customs revenue of Havana, 1789 to 1822—
Detail of revenue, 1824—Increase—Internal taxes, 1735 to 1818
—Revenue and expenditure, 1822—Comments of the Intendent—
Subsidies from Mexico to Cuba—[NOTE.—Sources of present
revenue examined—Maritime revenue and tariff—Internal taxes—
Direct revenue—State property—Declared revenue—Items of
government income to be added—Total revenue—Abuses in Cuba.
Evil effects of the revenue system—Appropriations—Civil list—
Army—Navy—Crown income—Average product to Spain—Per-
centage on official incomes—Revenue from 1826 to 1852—Com-
pared with revenue of Spanish government in Mexico—
Reflections.]

THE increase of agricultural prosperity in the
island of Cuba, and the accumulation of wealth
flowing from the value of its importations, has augmented the public revenue during late years to four
and a half, and perhaps even five millions of dollars.　The custom-house of Havana, which before
the year 1794 yielded less than $600,000, and from

1797 to 1800 an average of $1,900,000, brings to the public treasury, since the declaration of the freedom of commerce, a net sum of more than $3,100,000. As the colonial government gives the greatest publicity to everything concerning the collection of revenue in Cuba, we learn by the reports of the treasury department for the city and district of Havana, that from 1820 to 1825, the public revenue in the subordinate departments of this treasury, has oscillated between $3,200,000 and $3,400,000. If to this sum we add $800,000, which the treasury has received from other branches of revenue, as lottery, tithes, &c., and also the income from the custom-houses of Trinidad, Matanzas, Baracoa, and St. Jago de Cuba, which amounted to more than $600,000 previous to the year 1819, we are convinced that the estimated revenue of five millions of dollars for the whole island is not exaggerated. A few simple comparisons will prove how large is this product relatively to the actual state of the colony.

The island of Cuba has not over one forty-second part of the population of France, and as about one-half of its inhabitants live in a state of extreme poverty, they consume but little. Its revenues equal those of Colombia, and exceed the product of all the custom-houses of the United States prior to

the year 1795, when that Confederation had 4,500,000
inhabitants;[1] yet Cuba contains only 715,000. The
customs tariff is the principal source of revenue in
this beautiful colony; it produces more than three-
fifths of the total income, and suffices to cover with
ease, all the necessities of internal administration,
and military defence.

Though the disbursements of the treasury of
Havana have, during the last few years, exceeded
$4,000,000, this excessive expenditure has been
caused by the tenacious struggle which the metropolis has endeavored to sustain with the emancipated
colonies. Two millions of dollars have been dis-
bursed in the pay of troops and sailors, that have
retreated from the American continent to Spain by
way of Havana. All the while that Spain, ignoring
her true interests, shall delay the recognition of the
independence of the new republics, the island of
Cuba, menaced by Colombia and the Mexican Confederation, must maintain a military equipment in
self-defence, that will absorb the colonial revenues.
The navy alone stationed at Havana costs more than
$600,000, and the land forces require annually nearly

---

[1] The custom-houses of the United States, which, from 1801 to
1808 yielded sixteen millions annually, in 1816 gave only $7,282,000.
—*Morse's Modern Geography*, p. 638.—H.

a million and a half of dollars. Such a state of things cannot long endure, if Spain does not alleviate the burdens that weigh upon the colony.

From 1789, to 1797 the product of the custom-house at Havana never attained, one year with another, more than $700,000. The revenues contributed to the royal treasury were,

1789 .....$479,302	1793 .....$635,098 .
1790...... 642,720	1794...... 642,320
1791...... 520,202	1795...... 643,583
1792...... 849,904	1796...... 784,689

From 1797 to 1800 the crown and municipal duties collected at Havana amounted to $7,634,126, being an average of $1,908,000 :

1797 .....$1,257,017	1801 .....$2,170,970
1798...... 1,822,348	1802...... 2,400,932
1799...... 2,305,080	1803...... 1,637,465
1800...... 2,249,680	

The custom-house at Havana yielded in :

1808 .....$1,178,974	1811 .....$1,469,137
1809...... 1,913,605	1814...... 1,855,117
1810...... 1,292,619	

The decrease of revenue in 1808 was attributed to the American embargo, but in 1809 the court permitted the free entrance of foreign neutral vessels.

From 1815 to 1819 the crown duties collected at Havana amounted to $11,575,460; the municipal duties to $6,709,347, being a total of $18,284,807, and a yearly average of $3,657,000, of which the municipal duties composed fifty-six per cent. During the three succeeding years the income of the general treasury at Havana amounted to:

1820 .....$3,631,279   1822 .....$3,378,228
1821...... 3,277,639

In 1823, the crown and municipal duties on imports have yielded $2,734,563. The returns of the "Administracion General" of Havana for 1824, have been as follows:

I.—Import duties, ...$1,818,896
II.—Export duties, ...   326,816
III.—Coastwise duties, and other branches
    (salt, deposit, &c.),.............   188,415
IV.—Internal imposts—
    Tax on slaves, ...$ 73,109
    Tax on sales of land, ... 215,092
    Sub-administrations, ... 154,840
    Shops, :............... 19,714
    Other branches, ... 10,931
                            ————   473,686
V.—Auxiliary branches,................   136,923
VI.—Consulado, wharfage, &c., ...   80,564
       Total in 1824,.................$3,025,300

In the year 1825, the revenue of the city and district of Havana has amounted to $3,350,300.

These partial data demonstrate that from 1789 to 1824, the public revenue has increased seven fold. This fact is made more evident if we examine the returns of the ten subordinate treasuries of the interior—Matanzas, Villa Clara, Remedios, Trinidad, Santi Espiritu, Puerto Principe, Holguin, Bayamo, St. Jago de Cuba, and Baracoa. Señor Barrutia has published an interesting statement of these returns, embracing a period of eighty-three years, from 1735 to 1818. The revenue of these treasuries has progressively increased from $900 to $600,000.

1735	$896	1738	$1,794
1736	860	1739	4,747
1737	902		
Mean, for the five years,			1,840
1775	$123,246	1778	$158,624
1776	114,366	1779	146,007
1777	128,303	Mean,	133,315
1814	$317,699	1817	$524,442
1815	398,696	1818	618,036
1816	511,510	Mean,	474,072

The total amount for the eighty-three years is $13,098,000, of which St. Jago de Cuba contributed $4,390,000, Puerto Principe $2,224,000, and Matanzas $1 450,788.

By the returns of the general treasury, the public revenue of the district of Havana alone, in 1822, amounted to $4,311,862; of which $3,127,918 was from customs, $601,898 from items of direct income, as lottery, tithes, &c., and $581,978 drafts upon the fund of the .*Consulado* and deposits.

The expenditures during the same year were, for Cuba, $2,732,738, and for appropriations to maintain the struggle with the continental colonies, $1,362,062. In the first class we find $1,355,798 for the land forces charged with the defence of Havana, and contiguous towns, and $648,908 for the navy stationed at Havana. In the second class of expenditures, foreign to the local administration, we find $1,115,672 paid to 4,234 officers and soldiers, who, after having evacuated Mexico, Colombia, and other points of the the continent formerly under Spanish dominion, have passed through Havana on their return to Spain; and $164,000 expended in the defence of the castle of San Juan de Ulua.

Don Claudio Martinez de Pinillos, intendant of the island of Cuba, in his notes accompanying the report of the general treasury for 1822, makes the following observations: " If to the extraordinary expenditure of $1,362,022 for matters relating to the general interests of the Spanish monarchy, we add, on one hand, the greater part of the $648,908 appro-

priated to the royal navy, the service of which is not
limited to the defence of Havana, and, on the other
hand, the expenses arising from the visits of the
mail ships, and other vessels of war, we shall find
that $2,010,930 (which is nearly one-half the public
revenue) has been expended for purposes which
have no direct connection with the internal administration of the island." How much will be gained
by the welfare and enlightenment of that country,
if the day should arrive, when, enjoying internal
tranquillity, more than a million and a half of dollars
may be yearly employed in works of public utility.

In documents which I obtained from the archives
of the vice-royalty of Mexico, I have found that the
pecuniary assistance sent from the treasury of that
country annually to Havana, amounted, at the
beginning of the present century, to the following
sums :

For the squadron, navy-yards, and wants of
  the royal navy, by cedula of 16 Jan., 1790, $700,000
For the maritime establishments on the
  Mosquito coast, ...   40,000
For the army of Havana, ... 290,000
For the same at St. Jago de Cuba,......... 146,000
For fortifications,.. 150,000
For the purchase of tobacco and segars for
  the royal factory at Sevilla, ... 500,000
                                        ———
                                    $1,826,000

To this sum, which is now borne by the treasury at Havana, we may add $577,000 which Mexico paid to the treasury of Louisiana, $151,000 to that of Florida, and $377,000 to the island of Puerto Rico.

[NOTE.—Before proceeding to examine the present state of the revenue in Cuba, a succinct view of the sources from which it is derived, may not be inappropriate here. For greater clearness, we shall class them under four heads :—I. Maritime revenue, being that collected by customs, imposts upon exports, imports, and shipping; II. Internal taxes, comprising fixed and stated imposts; III. Direct revenue, being that collected not by imposts, under variable conditions; IV. State property, being income from property belonging to the crown.

I. MARITIME REVENUE.—The tariff on imports is arranged with a fixed per centage upon a stated valuation of nearly all the articles of commerce. Inspectors examine and class the importations, for the collection of the proper duties, and where the tariff does not state the valuation, they appraise the article. The principle adopted for valuation by the tariff, seems to be that of attaining as nearly as possible the market value of the articles in Havana, exclusive only of the duties thereon; and as a general rule, the per centage is arranged upon the following scale, although there are some few exceptions. Cotton and woolen goods and articles of food, 35½ per cent.; linen and silk goods, and articles of use, 29½ per cent. These are the rates for foreign products imported in foreign bottoms. When of Spanish product or manufacture, imported from Spain, the same goods pay only 9½ per cent. duty, and there is also a differential duty on goods of foreign product or manufacture, of 10 per cent. on the first, and 8 per cent. on the second class, in favor of importations in Spanish bottoms. A few articles pay fixed duties, such as flour, which from Spain pays $2, and from foreign ports $10 75 a barrel.

The tariff upon exports is in most instances a fixed arbitrary impost, having no relation to the value of the goods; for instance, sugar pays 87½ cents a box, coffee 20 cents a quintal, segars 75 cents a thousand, &c. The tonnage duties are levied at the rate of 62½ cents a ton for Spanish, and $1 50 per ton for foreign vessels, according to Spanish measurement. There are several other small tonnage imposts, as health, dredging, &c., and fees and dues for visits, clearance, lights, &c. Under the warehouse or bonded system, goods entered and cleared in bond

15

pay 1¼ per cent. entry, the same for clearance, and 1¼ per cent. storage yearly, after the first year. Materials for railroads, machinery for sugar estates, books and instruments for scientific institutions, and a small number of other articles are free of duty.

II. INTERNAL TAXES.—The principal items of this class of revenue are the following:—

Alcabala, a tax of six per cent. on the value of real estate and slaves sold or transferred. There is also an additional tax of six per cent. on the amount of the *alcabala*, which is imposed under certain circumstances. The annual yield of this impost varies between $600,000 and $700,000.

Meats consumed.—A tax of $3 50 per head on all beef cattle, 37½ cents for each sheep or goat, and 31¼ cents for each arrobe of swine killed for consumption, and 12¼ cents per arrobe on all meat killed for drying or curing purposes. The annual yield of this tax varies from $500,000 to $600,000.

Tithes.—Ten per cent. on the product of the haciendas, potreros, and all small cattle breeding or labor farms. Two-and-a-half per cent. on the product of sugar, coffee, and tobacco plantations. The annual yield of this tax to the government varies from $400,000 to $500,000.

Stamps.—An impost raised by the obligatory use

of stamped paper in all official intercourse (except diplomatic), tribunals, public instruments, bills of exchange, promissory notes, &c. The paper for common uses, is·divided into six classes, the price for each sheet being for the first, $8; second, $6; third, $1 50; fourth, 50 cents; fifth (for official intercourse), and sixth (for the declared pauper), 5 cents each. This tax produces from $250,000 to $300,000. The *stamps* for bills of exchange and notes, are graduated at 18¾ cents for $250 and under; 37½ cents for $625 and under; 75 cents for $1,250 and under, and 75 cents for each additional $1,250. The annual product from this tax is between $35,000 and $45,000, in addition to the above stated product from other stamps.

Judicial Fees.—The judges of the *Real Audiencia*, and the *Alcaldes Mayores* having a fixed salary, the fees accruing to them are paid into the royal treasury, and yield to it from $50,000 to $55,000 yearly.

Tax on Costs.—A tax of four per cent. on all assessed costs of judicial proceedings, yields annually from $50,000 to $70,000.

Shops and Stores.—A fixed impost of $30 each, in Havana, and $25 in other parts of the island, yielding from $125,000 to $150,000 annually.

Mortgages.—A tax of one-half of one per cent. on

the value of all property sold is collected through
the registrar of mortgages; yielding from $40,000 to
$50,000, per annum.

There are several minor imposts, as tax on cock-
pits, yielding from $20,000 to $30,000—on house
servants, water tax at Havana, *novenos reales*, auction
tax, &c.

III. DIRECT REVENUE.—Includes items of direct
income to the treasury, which are not taxes, among
which the principal are:

Lottery.—Carried on by the government, which
reserves twenty-five per cent. of the gross amount of
each scheme. It is drawn every three weeks, and
yields annually from $650,000 to $670,000.

Post-Office.—Yields a net annual revenue of about
$100,000.

Fees of the Captain-General.—These fees are by
law to be paid into the treasury; but in the returns
for the year 1853 (the latest we possess), the amount
is not stated. Well-informed persons suppose it to
amount to $100,000, and some place it as high as
two or three times this sum.

Fines, Confiscations, &c.—Are payable directly
into the treasury, but they cannot be estimated.

IV. STATE PROPERTY.—The property of the State

in Cuba yields an income naturally variable. It arises principally from the following sources:

Church Property.—The administration of the expropriated church property, and occasional partial sales, produces a regular income. In 1850, it amounted to about $200,000.

Rentals.—Rents of State lands and property yields from $40,000 to $50,000 annually.

Land Sales.—The sales of public lands in 1850, produced $37,000.

Church Revenues, expropriated by the State, yield in the same year $87,000.

There are some minor branches of income which brings up the annual yield of this class to about $400,000.

The declared revenue of the Spanish government in Cuba, in 1852, the latest of which we have been able to obtain complete returns, was as follows:

I. Maritime revenue,	$8,870,000
II. Internal taxes,	2,750,000
III. Direct revenue,	980,000
IV. State property,	400,000
	$13,000,000

But in order to arrive at a knowledge of the approximate amount of government exactions in

Cuba, we should add to the foregoing the following items, which are properly state burdens, and constitute revenue.

Tax on slaves imported—for which $51 each is collected by officials—yearly average, 10,000, .		$510,000
Municipal revenues of the several ayuntamientos, and municipalities in the island, ...		600,000
Income of the non-salaried administrative officers of the government—two Governors (of Matanzas and St. Jago), $25,000 each, ...	$ 50,000	
29 Lieut. Governors, at $5,000, ...	145,000	
299 Captains de Partido at $1,000, ...	299,000	
Subordinate officers, ...	326,000	
		820,000
Income of non-salaried judiciary officers :		
42 Alcaldes ordinarios, at $5,000, ...	$210,000	
100 Assessors (crown law officers), at $5,000, ...	500,000	
450 Subordinate officers of courts, at $800, ...	360,000	
		1,070,000
Income of non-salaried officials, ...$		3,000,000
Revenue before stated, ...		13,000,000
Total revenue, ...$		16,000,000

This estimate does not pretend to include all the exactions to which the people of Cuba are subjected by the officials of the present government, but only the pay of those administrative and judiciary officers, who, under proper systems of government, are paid fixed salaries by the State, in order to prevent as far as possible, an abuse of the power they must necessarily wield in the community. To show the character and extent of this abuse, we copy the following extract from Gen. Concha's work on Cuba, published in Madrid, in 1853:

"The absence of fixed salaries makes official situations uncertain in the extreme, under which the probabilities of their proving lucrative can only be estimated by antecedents. What, then, must any one think, calculate, or hope for, who, soliciting or accepting an appointment, sees that after a few years an incumbent returns to Spain with a fortune, not such as he might have made by means of the strictest economy, while holding one of the best paid places at home, but one comparable only to those made by fortunate speculators. * * * * For many reasons, it is unfortunately too notorious that an officer of a special tribunal was able to save or make from his office, in the short space of four months, more than FORTY THOUSAND DOL-LARS!"[1]

The appropriation of the revenue of Cuba, as

---

[1] "Memoria sobre el Estado político de Cuba, por Gen. José de la Concha," p. 331.

nearly as it can be made up from the returns of the Havana treasury, is as follows:

CIVIL LIST.

Pay and expenses of executive officers, $	250,000
Perquisites of same,	1,330,000
Pay and expenses of judiciary,	110,000
Perquisites of same,	1,070,000
Municipal expenditures,	600,000
Junta de Fomento, public works,	350,000
Church service,	200,000
Government police, $75,000	
Civil do. 90,000	
	165,000
Civil pensions, $130,000	
Church, do. 120,000	
Heirs of Columbus, do., 16,000	
	166,000
Public charities,	33,000
Public schools,	12,000
Prisons,	65,000
Pay and expenses of treasury,	740,000
Balances to other treasuries,	510,000
Difference between the gross amount of revenue, as returned in the "Balanzas de Comercio," and net revenue declared,	2,079,000
	$7,680,000

ARMY LIST.

Pay roll of

19 Reg., 4 comp. Infantry, ...$1,790,000	
2 Regiments, Cavalry, ...	210,000
1 Reg., 5 comp. Artillery,........	380,000
General officers, ...	53,000
Engineer corps, ...	86,000
	————$2,429,000

Clothing, equipment, and arms,...............	90,000
Cattle and equipment,.	230,000
Material for artillery corps,..................	155,000
Ditto " engineer do., ...	125,000
Transportation, ...	150,000
Other expenditures for the army, ...	100,000
Hospitals,..................................	300,000
Military pensions, ...	155,000
Pay roll of Militia Infantry, ...$12,000	
do. do. Cavalry, ... 53,000	
	65,000
	$3,799,000

NAVY LIST.

Pay roll, and expenses of ships, dockyards, &c., $1,750,000

REVENUE TO THE CROWN.

Drafts of the general treasury at Madrid, ...$2,450,000	
Annual remittance to Maria Christina,.........	166,000
Interest on drafts from Spain,................	22,000
Spanish ministers and consuls in America,......	117,000
Annual remittance of segars for the court, ...	16,000
	$2,771,000

RECAPITULATION.

Civil List,... ....$7,680,000
Army List,... 3,799,000
Navy List, ... 1,750,000
Revenue to the Crown, ... 2,771,000
                                 _____
                                 $16,000,000

The net income to the crown of Spain from the
island of Cuba, it will be seen, is about two and
three quarters millions. The published returns show
that from 1836 to 1850 it averaged about two millions eight hundred thousand dollars. While this
revenue flows into the coffers of the State, the
administration proper has another source of revenue
in Cuba, in the percentage upon the product of their
offices which many officers in that island pay to the
officers in power in the mother country, that they
may retain their places.

Baron Humboldt has given, in the preceding pages,
a succinct view of the declared revenue of Cuba to
1825, to which we can add the following, compiled
from the works of Don Ramon de la Sagra, the
" Cuadro Estadistico," and several " Balanzas," in
our possession :

1826 to 1830 ....$42,808,182
1831 " 1835 43,373,087
1836 " 1840 50,650,982
                  Carry forward.... $136,832,251

```
                   Brought forward... . $186,832,251
 1841 " 1845 ........................ 54,465,970
 1846 " 1850 (approximate) ............ 57,500,000
          1851¹ .... ................. 12,462,834
          1852 ........................ 12,873,086
                               Total........ $274,134,241
```

A comparison of the foregoing views of the revenue of the Spanish government in Cuba, with its
revenue in the vice-royalty of Mexico in 1809, the
year in which the revolution began, may not be unin-
teresting.   General Zavala, in his " Ensayo Historico
de la Revolucion de Mexico," states the revenues of
the vice-royalty in detail, which reduced to a tabular form, exhibit the following figures :

REVENUE.

Mexico.		Cuba.	
I. Mining revenue,	$3,837,954	I. Maritime revenue,	$8,870,000
II. Internal taxes,	5,793,064	II. Internal taxes,	2,750,000
III. Direct revenue,	1,487,116	III. Direct revenue,	980,000
IV. Tobacco monopoly,	3,927,822	IV. State property,	400,000
	$15,045,956		$13,000,000

¹ In estimating the revenue for 1851 and 1852, we have added to
the maritime revenue, as given by the " Balanzas " for those years,
an estimated revenue of four millions from other sources.

EXPENDITURES.

Mexico.		Cuba.	
I. Civil list,	not stated	I. Civil list,	—— ——
II. Army and Navy,	$3,800,000	II. Army and Navy,	$5,549,000
III. Judiciary & Church,	250,000	III. Judiciary & Church,	310,000
IV. Pensions,	200,000	IV. Pensions,	321,000
V. Hospitals,	400,800	V. Hospitals,	300,000
VI. Treasury expenses,	596,260	VI. Treasury expenses,	740,000
VII. Interest,	1,496,000	VII. Interest,	22,000
	$6,743,060		$7,242,000

These data show that the financial condition of the government of Cuba at the present time, and that of the Spanish government in Mexico at the time of its greatest prosperity, are very similar; but we should remember that the population of the two countries at the relative periods of time is widely dissimilar, that of Cuba being a million and a half, and that of Mexico seven millions.

The system under which this enormous sum of sixteen millions of dollars is extracted from less than a million and a half of people, exercises, apart from its large amount, a very pernicious influence upon the public welfare. The imposts upon food, and articles of common use, by the tariff on imports, and the tax on meats killed in the country, throw more than sixty per cent. of the declared revenue directly upon the labor of the country, while the system of non-paid officials and officers of justice, tends to throw the burden of their support upon the poor, it being notorious that the wealthy can obtain favor by personal influence. Thus, nearly the whole burden of the State is thrown upon the common people, which tends to accumulate wealth in the hands of the few, making the rich richer, and the poor poorer, to the manifest disadvantage of the common weal.

With such a buoyant prosperity, what might we not hope from Cuba, if the millions which are now drawn from the fountains of her wealth to support a foreign and corrupt government, and a large non-producing armed force, were allowed to flow in their natural channels, to the reward of labor, the increase of individual wealth, and the advance of the public welfare.]

CHAPTER XIII.

A TRIP TO TRINIDAD.

Change of plans—Preparations for departure—Remission of specimens to Europe—Long absence without letters—Joyful news—
Difficulties to be surmounted—Objections met—Charter of a
schooner—Financial arrangements—Departure—Grateful acknowledgments—The Orleans princes—Road across the island—Cotton plant—Batabanó—Supposed encroachments of the sea—
Gloom of the marshes—Cocodrilos and Caymans—Their habits
and characteristics—Specimens—Comparison with those of South
America—Suggestions—Dampier's description of them—Embar-
cation—Discomfort on board—Gulf of Batabanó—Isle of Pines
—Jardines and Jardinillos—Struggle of Columbus here—Beautiful phenomenon—Temperatures of the sea—Clearness of the water
—Cause thereof—Incompetency of pilot—Anchor at night—
Multitude of shooting-stars—Absence of life in these regions—
Contrast with the time of Columbus—Arts of the Indian fishermen—Similar arts among other uncivilized nations—Visit to the
Cays—Their geognostic constitution—Does the sea grow shallow
here—Cay Bonito—Pelicans—Barbarity of the sailors—Vegeta-
tion—Charm of these regions—Memories of Columbus and Cortés
Columbus and the natives—Fleets of pirogues from Yucatan—
Hopes of Columbus—His remarkable vision—His pathetic complaints—Hernan Cortés—Stranding of his ship—Gathering of his
fleet—Fall of Mexico—Strange vicissitudes—Cay Flamenco—

Fresh water on the Cays—Springs in the sea—Similar springs at
Cardenas—The Manatee—Dampier's description of it—Cay de
Piedras—The open sea—Its temperature—Marshy coast—Las
Casas grant of Indians—Bay of Jagua—Cienfuegos—Hills of San
Juan—A bold coast—Mexican wax found in Cuba—River San
Juan—Remains of native inhabitants—Sea temperature—Arrival
at the river Guaurabo—Ludicrous conveyance to the city—
Trinidad—Absence of snow—First settlement—Fine view—Astro-
nomical observations—Hospitality—Dinner given by the governor
—Complaints of the inhabitants—Ports of Trinidad, Guaurabo—
Casilda—An agreeable evening—Cuban ladies—Departure from
Trinidad—Stately conveyance—Fire-flies—Interesting anecdote
—Conclusion.

TOWARD the close of April,[1] 1801, Monsieur
Bonpland and myself, having completed the series of
observations we had proposed making on the extreme
northern limit of the torrid zone, were about to
depart for Vera Cruz with the squadron of Admiral
Aristizabal; but the false intelligence contained in
the public gazettes, relative to the expedition of
Captain Baudin, induced us to abandon the project
we had entertained, of crossing Mexico on our way
to the Philippine Islands. Many papers, and particularly those of the United States, announced that

---

[1] Thus, in the original, but it is undoubtedly a slip of the pen,
and should read February instead of "April." Baron Humboldt
arrived at Havana, on his first visit to Cuba, on the 19th December,
1800, and sailed from Trinidad on the 16th March, 1801.

two French corvettes, the *Géographe* and the *Natu-
raliste*, had sailed for Cape Horn, and would run
along the coasts of Chili and Peru, from whence
they were to proceed to New Holland.

This news excited me greatly, for it again filled'
my imagination with the projects I had formed during my stay in Paris, when I had not ceased for a
moment to urge the ministry of the Directory to
hasten the departure of Captain Baudin. While on
the point of leaving Spain, I had promised to join
the expedition wherever I might be able to reach it.
When one desires a thing that may produce unto-
ward results, he easily persuades himself that a sense
of obligation is the only motive that influences his
determination. Monsieur Bonpland, always enterprising and confident in our good fortune, determined
at once to divide our collection of plants into three
parts.

In order not to expose all that we had collected,
with so much labor, on the banks of the Orinoco,
Atabapo, and Rio Negro, to the chances of a long
sea voyage, we sent one part to Germany by way
of England, another to France by way of Cadiz;
and left the third at Havana. We afterwards had
reason to congratulate ourselves on the adoption of
this course, which prudence counselled. Each part
contained, with slight difference, the same species

and classes, and no precaution was omitted to secure the remission of the cases to Sir Joseph Banks, or to the directors of the Museum of Natural History at Paris, in case they should fall into the hands of English or French cruisers.

Fortunately, the manuscripts which I had at first intended to send with the portion sent to Cadiz, were not placed in charge of our friend and fellow-traveller, friar Juan Gonzalez. This estimable young man, of whom I have often had occasion to speak, had accompanied us to Havana, on his way to Spain, and sailed from Cuba shortly after our departure; but the vessel in which he embarked was lost with all her passengers and freight, in a tempest on the coast of Africa. By this shipwreck we lost one of the duplicates of our collection of plants; and also, which was a greater misfortune for the cause of science, all the insects that Bonpland had gathered, under a thousand difficulties, during our voyage to the Orinoco and Rio Negro.

By an extraordinary fatality we remained two years in the Spanish colonies without receiving a single letter from Europe, and those which reached us in the three subsequent years, gave no information in regard to the collections we had sent. One will readily conceive how anxious I was to learn the fate of a diary which contained all our astronomical

observations, and barometrical readings of altitudes,
and which I had so patiently copied out in full.   It
was only after having traversed New Granada,
Mexico, and Peru, and when I was on the point of
leaving the New World, that in the public library
at Philadelphia, I accidentally ran my eye over the
table of contents of a scientific review, and there
saw these words, "Arrival of the Manuscripts of
M. Humboldt, at the residence of his brother, in
Paris, by way of Spain."   With difficulty I suppressed the expression of my joy, and it seemed to
me that no table of contents had ever before been so
well arranged.

While M. Bonpland labored night and day,
dividing and arranging our collections, I had the
ungracious task of meeting a thousand obstacles that
presented themselves to our sudden and unforeseen
departure.   There was no vessel in the harbor of
Havana that would convey us to Porto Bello or
Carthagena, and the persons whom I consulted took
a pleasure in exaggerating the inconveniences that
attended the crossing of the isthmus, and the delays
incident to a voyage southward, from Panama to
Guayaquil, and thence to Lima or Valparaiso.

They censured me, and perhaps with reason, for
not continuing to explore the vast and rich countries
of Spanish America, which had been closed for

half a century to foreign travellers. The vicissitudes of a voyage round the world, touching only at a few islands, or the arid coasts of a continent, did not seem to them preferable to studying the geological constitution of New Spain, which alone contributed five-eighths of the mass of silver taken yearly from all the mines of the known world. To these arguments, I opposed the wish to determine on a large scale, the inflexion of the curves of equal inclination of the decrease of the magnetic force from the pole toward the equator, and the temperature of the ocean as it varies with the latitude, the direction of the currents, and the proximity of banks and shoals.

In proportion as obstacles rose to my plans, I hastened the more to put them in execution, and not being able to find a passage in a neutral vessel, I chartered a Catalan schooner lying in the roadstead of Batabanó, to take me to Porto Bello or Carthagena, as the winds might permit. The extended relations of the prosperous commerce of Havana afforded me the means for making my pecuniary arrangements for several years. General Gonzalo de O'Farril, distinguished alike for his talents and his high character, then resided in my own country, as minister from the court of Spain. I was enabled to exchange my income in Prussia for a part of his in the island of Cuba, and the family of Don

Ygnacio O'Farril y Herrera, his brother, kindly did all they could to forward my projects at the time of my unexpected departure from Havana.

On the sixth of March, we learned that the schooner I had chartered was ready for sea. The road to Batabanó led us again through Güines, to the sugar plantation of Rio Blanco, the residence of Count de Jaruco y Mopox, which was adorned with all the luxuries that good taste and a large fortune can command. That hospitality which generally wanes as civilization advances, is still practised in Cuba with the same profusion as in the most distant countries of Spanish America. We naturalists and simple travellers accord with pleasure to the inhabitants of Havana, the same grateful acknowledgments that have been given to them by those illustrious strangers,[1] who, everywhere that I have followed their route, have left in the New World the remembrance of their noble simplicity, their ardor for learning and their love for the public weal.

From Rio Blanco to Batabanó, the road passes through an uncultivated country, a portion of which

[1] The young princes of the House of Orleans (the Duke d'Orleans, the Duke de Montpensier, and the Count de Beaujolois), who visited the United States and Havana, descending the Ohio and Mississippi rivers, and remained a year in the island of Cuba.—H.

contains many springs. In the open spaces the indigo and cotton plants grow wild for want of cultivation. As the capsule of the *Gossipium* opens at that season of the year when the northern storms are most frequent, the fibre which surrounds the seed is torn from side to side, and the cotton, which in other respects is of the best quality, suffers greatly when the period of the storms coincides with its ripening. Further south we found a new species of the palm, with fan-like leaves (*corifa maritima*), having a free filament in the interstices between the leaves. This corifa abounds through a portion of the southern coast, and takes the place of the majestic royal palm, and the *coco crispa* of the northern shore. Porous limestone (of the Jurassic formation) appeared from time to time in the plain.

Batabanó was at this time a poor hamlet, where a church had been built a few years before. Half a league beyond it the swamp begins, which extends to the entrance of the Bay of Jagua, a distance of seventy leagues from west to east. It is supposed at Batabanó that the sea continues its encroachments upon the land, and that the oceanic irruption has been observed particularly at the time of the great upheaving at the close of the eighteenth century, when the tobacco mills near Havana were destroyed, and the course of the river Chorrera was changed.

Nothing can be more gloomy than the view of the marshes around Batabanó, for not a tree breaks the monotony of the scene, and the decaying trunks of a few palms only rise, like broken masts, in the midst of great thickets of running vines and purple flag flowers.

As we remained only one night at Batabanó, I regretted that I could not obtain exact information relative to the two species of *cocodrilos* that infest the swamp. The inhabitants call one the *cayman*, and the other the *cocodrilo*, which name is generally applied to both. We were assured that the latter is the most agile, and the tallest when on its feet; that its snout runs to a much sharper point than that of the cayman, with which it never associates. It is very fearless, and is even said to leap on board of vessels when it can find a support for its tail. The great daring of this animal was noticed during the early expeditions of Diego Velasquez. At the river Cauto, and along the marshy coast of Jagua, it will wander a league from the sea-shore to devour the hogs in the fields. Some attain a length of fifteen feet, and the most savage of them will, it is said, chase a man on horseback like the wolves of Europe —while those that are known as *caymanes* at Batabanó, are so timid that the people do not fear to bathe in waters where they dwell in droves.

These habits, and the name of *cocodrilo*, which is given in Cuba to the most dangerous of the carnivorous saurians, seem to me to indicate a different species from the great animals of the Orinoco and Magdalena rivers, and St. Domingo. The colonists in all other parts of Spanish America, deceived by the exaggerated tales of the ferocity of the Egyptian crocodile, affirm that there are no true crocodiles except in the Nile; while zoologists have found in America the *cayman*, with obtuse snout and no scales on his legs, and the *cocodrilo*, with pointed snout and with scales on his legs. At the same time we find on the old continent, the common crocodile, and those of the Ganges, with rounded snout.

The *crocodilus acutus* of St. Domingo, which I cannot now undertake to class specifically, and the *cocodrilo* of the great Orinoco and Magdalena rivers, have, in the words of Cuvier, so admirable a resemblance to the crocodile of the Nile, that it has been necessary to examine minutely every part, in order to show that the law of Buffon, relative to the distribution of species in the tropical regions of the two continents, was not defective.

As on my second visit to Havana, in 1804, I could not revisit the marshes of Batabanó, I procured at a great expense specimens of the two species, which the inhabitants call cayman and cocodrilo.

Two of the latter reached Havana alive, the oldest being about four feet three inches long. Their capture had been very difficult, and they were brought to the city muzzled, tied upon the back of a jack-mule. They were strong and ferocious, and in order to observe their habits and movements, we put them in a large room, where, from the top of a high table, we could see them attacked by dogs.

Having been for six months on the Orinoco, Apure, and Magdalena rivers, in the midst of coco-drilos, we observed with renewed pleasure, before our return to Europe, these singular animals, that pass with an astonishing rapidity from a state of complete immobility to the most impetuous motion. Those which were sent to us from Batabanó as coco-drilos, had the snout as pointed as those of the Orinoco and Magdalena (*Crocodilus acutus*, Cuv.); their color was somewhat darker, being a blackish-green on the back, and white on the belly, with yellow spots on the sides. I counted thirty-eight teeth in the upper, and thirty in the lower jaw, as in the true crocodile. Of the upper teeth, the ninth and tenth, and of the lower, the first and fourth, were the largest. The description which Bonpland and myself made on the spot at Costa Firma, expressly states that the fourth lower tooth projects freely over the upper jaw; the posterior extremities were flattened. These cocodrilos of Batabanó, seemed to us, specifically the same with the crocodilus acutus, although it is true that what we were told of its habits, does not accord with what we ourselves had observed on the Orinoco; but the carnivorous saurians of like species, and in the same river, are mild and timid, or ferocious and fearless, according to the nature of the locality.

The animal called cayman at Batabanó, died on the way to Havana, and those in charge had not the foresight to bring the body to us, so that we were not able to compare the two species. Are there, perhaps, on the south side of Cuba true caymans, with the rounded snout, and the fourth under tooth entering the upper jaw; and another species (alligators), like those of Florida? In view of the assertions of the colonists relative to the more pointed head of the cocodrilo of Batabanó, this is almost certain. If this is the case, the people of the island have made, by a happy instinct, a distinction between the cocodrilo and the cayman, with all the exactitude now used by zoologists in separating families that belong to the same genera, and bear the same name.

I do not doubt that the sharp-snouted cocodrilo, and the alligator or flat-nosed cayman do not live together, but in distinct bands, on the marshy shores

between the bay of Jagua, Batabanó, and the isle of
Pines. It was at the latter that Dampier, so worthy
of eulogy as a physiological observer and intrepid
sailor, perceived clearly the great difference'between
the cayman and the American cocodrilo. His statements on this point, in his voyage to the bay of
Campeachy, might have excited the curiosity of the
learned a century since, if zoologists would not so
often reject, with disdain, the observations of navigators, and other travellers, who do not possess
scientific attainments, relative to animals. Dampier,
after having noticed many of the characteristics,
though not all with equal exactitude, that distinguish
the cocodrilo from the cayman, insists upon the
geographical distribution of these enormous saurians.

"In the bay of Campeachy," he says, "I have
seen only caymans or alligators; in the island of
Gran Cayman there are cocodrilos, and no alligators; in the isle of Pines, and in the numerous
creeks of the coast of Cuba, there are cocodrilos
and caymans together." To these precious observations of Dampier I will add, that the true cocodrilo
(*C. acutus*) is also found in the Leeward Islands,
which are near to Costa Firma, as, for example,
Trinidad, Margarita, and probably also in Curaçoa,
notwithstanding the scarcity of fresh water. It is

also found further south (but I have never found
with them any of the species of alligators that
abound on the coast of Guiana), in the Neverí,
Magdalena, Apure, and the Orinoco, to the conflu-
ence of the Casiquiaro with the Rio Negro (lat.
2° 2′), which is more than four hundred leagues
from Batabanó. It would be important to determine the limits of the several species of carnivorous
saurians, on the eastern shore of Guatemala and
Mexico, between the Mississippi river and Chagres.

Before sunrise, on the ninth of March, we were
under way, somewhat intimidated by the extremely
small size of our schooner, on board of which we
could lie down only upon deck. The well-like cabin
received air and light from above, and barely
afforded room for our instruments; in it the thermometer stood constantly at 32° or 33° c. (90° or
92° F.). Fortunately, these inconveniences lasted
only twenty days, and the navigation of the
Orinoco in canoes, and a passage at sea on board of
an American vessel laden with beef which had
been dried in the sun, had taught us not to be too
delicate.

The Gulf of Batabanó, surrounded by low and
marshy coasts, seems like a vast desert. The fisher
birds, which generally are found at their posts before
the land birds, and the lazy *samurros* are awake,

are only occasionally seen. The water of the sea has
a dark green color, as in some of the lakes of Switzer-
land, while the sky, from the great purity of the
atmosphere, had from the first appearance of the
sun, that clear blue so much admired by landscape
painters in the south of Italy; and through the pure
air the most distant objects stood forth to the view
with an extraordinary brilliancy.

Our schooner was the only vessel in the gulf, for
none enter the roadstead of Batabanó but smugglers,
or, as they are called, with greater courtesy, "the traders." I have mentioned before, when speaking of the
project of a canal through Güines, how important Batabanó might become to the trade between Cuba and
Venezuela. In its present state there are barely nine
feet of water, as no attempt has been made to deepen
it. The port is at the bottom of a bay formed by
Punta Gorda on the east, and Punta de Salinas on the
west; but the bay itself is only the concave side of
a great gulf, which is fourteen leagues deep from
north to south, closed by an innumerable number of
cays and banks for a distance of fifty leagues, from
the bay of Cortéz to Cay de Piedras.

Within this labyrinth there rises one large island
only, the area of which is four times greater than
Martinique, and whose arid hills are crowned with
majestic pines. This is the Isle of Pines, named the

"Evangelist" by Columbus, and the island of Santa Maria by other navigators of the sixteenth century. It is célebrated for the excellent mahogany which it produces.

We sailed east-southeast through the Don Cristobal channel, to make the rocky shores of Cay de Piédras, and clear the archipelago which the Spanish pilots, from the earliest times of the conquest, have called the *Jardines* and *Jardinillos*. The true *Jardines de la Reina* (the Queen's gardens), nearer to Cape Cruz, are divided from the archipelago which I am about to describe, by thirty-five leagues of open sea. Columbus gave them this name in 1494, when, during his second voyage, he was fifty-eight days struggling with the winds and currents between the Isle of Pines and the eastern cape of Cuba. He described these islands as being "green, filled with trees, and very beautiful."

And in truth a portion of these misnamed gardens is very beautiful, for the voyager varies the scene momently, and the verdure of some of the islets borrows a new splendor from the contrast with others that present to the eye only white and arid sands. The surface of these, heated by the rays of the sun, seems to undulate as though it were water, and by the contact with the strata of air of unequal tempera-

ture, produces from ten in the morning until four in
the afternoon, all the varied phenomena of the
mirage. In those desert solitudes it is the sun that
animates the landscape, giving motion to the objects
that glitter under his rays; the dusty plain, the trunks
of trees, and the rocks jutting out into the sea.
From the time of his rising these inert masses seem
suspended in the air, and the sandy beaches present
the deceitful spectacle of a watery plain gently agitated by the wind. A shred of cloud suffices to
throw down alike, the trunks of trees and the suspended rocks, to still the undulating surface of the
plain, and to dissipate those charms which the Arabian, Persian, and Indian poets, have celebrated in
song as "the sweet illusions of the desert solitude."

We doubled Cape Matahambre very slowly. As
the chronometer of Louis Berthoud had kept time
well in Havana, I improved the opportunity to determine, on that and the following days, the positions
of the Don Cristobal, Flamenco, Diego Perez, and
Piedras cays. I also found occupation in examining
the influence of the varying depth upon the temperature of the surface water. Sheltered by so many
islets the surface is always calm, as if it were a lake
of fresh water; the strata of different depths do not

mingle with each other, and yet the slightest change in the soundings influence the thermometer.[1]

I was surprised to find that east of the small cay Don Cristobal, the deep soundings are not marked by the milky color of the water, as is the case on Shark Shoals south of Jamaica, and in many other places where I have observed with the thermometer. The bottom of the Gulf of Batabanó is a sand of decomposed coral, bearing sea-wreck that barely reaches to the surface. The water is greenish, as we have already noted, and the absence of the milky color arises, without doubt, from the perfect calm that reigns in these places; for wherever the water is agitated to a certain depth, a very fine sand, or the particles of limestone held suspended in the water, make it turgid and give it the milky tinge. Yet there are shoals which are not distinguished either by the color or the lower temperature of the sea, and

[1] I observed the following readings by Reaumer's thermometer :

Sea.	Air.	Depth.	
19°.7	22°.3	10 feet.	Eight miles N. of Punta Gorda.
18°.8	23°.0	7½ "	Between Las Gordas and Don Cristobal Cays.
19°.7	23°.3	10 "	Near Cay Flamenco.
20°.7	22°.0	80 "	Deep soundings between Cay Flamenco and Cay de Piedras.
19°.6	24°.3	9 "	Eastern margin of same, very near Cay de Piedras.
18°.3	24°.3	8 "	A little further east.
21°.5	23°.0	—	No bottom south of Jagua. H.

I believe these phenomena result from the nature of
a hard and rocky bottom, without sand or coral,
from the form and inclination of the foundations, the
velocity of the currents, and the absence of a com-
municating motion in the lower strata of water.
The low temperature generally indicated by the
thermometer, on the surface of deep water, arises
from the sinking of the heated particles caused by
their diffusive movement and nocturnal cooling, and
by the mingling of the deep strata which rise along
the sides of the banks, as upon an inclined plain, to
unite with the surface waters.

Notwithstanding the small size of our craft, and
the much praised skill of our pilot, we grounded
very often; but as the bottom was soft, we incurred
no danger. Yet at sunset it was thought best to
anchor near the outlet of the Don Cristobal channel.
The sky was admirably clear during the first part of
the night, and we saw a multitude of shooting stars
landward of us, all passing in the same direction,
counter to the east wind which then prevailed in the
lower portions of the atmosphere. The solitude of
these regions differs widely now from their appearance in the time of Columbus, when they were
inhabited, and frequented by large numbers of
fishermen. The natives of Cuba then availed themselves of a small sucker-fish to catch the large sea-

turtle, tying a long cord to the tail of the *reves*, a name which the Spaniards gave to this small member of the Echeneis genera.

This *fisher-fish* fastens itself to the shell of the turtle, which abound in the narrow and winding channels of the Jardinillos, by a flat disc surrounded with suckers, which it bears upon its head. Columbus says, "the *reves* will suffer itself to be torn to pieces rather than be forced to lose any body of which it has taken hold." Thus, with the same cord, the Indians drew forth the fisher-fish and the turtle. When Gomara and Pedro Martir de Angliera, the learned secretary of Charles V., related to Europe this fact which they had learned from the lips of the companions of Columbus, it was believed to be only a traveller's tale.

We now know by the evidence of Captain Rogers, of Dampier, and Commerson, that this same artifice, which was used in the Jardinillos, is practised by the inhabitants of the eastern coast of Africa near Cape Natal, in Mozambique and in Madagascar. In Egypt, in St. Domingo, and in the lakes of Mexico, men were accustomed to cover their heads with large perforated gourds, and lying with their bodies in the water, caught the water fowl by their feet as they swam upon its surface. The Chinese have availed themselves from the most remote antiquity,

16*

of birds of the pelican family, for the purpose of
fishing on the shores, placing rings around their
necks to prevent their swallowing the prize and thus
fishing only for themselves. In the lower grades of
civilization, all the sagacity of man is displayed in
the artifices of the chase and fishery. Nations that
probably have never communicated with each other,
present the most palpable analogies in the means they
adopt to subdue the animal creation.

Three days passed before we could emerge from
the labyrinth of the Jardines and Jardinillos. We
were every night at anchor, and during the day
visited those islets or cays, where we could most
easily land. As we advanced toward the east, the
sea become less smooth, and we began to recognize
the shallows by the milky color of the water. Upon
the margin of a kind of whirlpool which exists
between Cay Flamenco and Cay de Piedras, we
found that the temperature of the sea at the surface,
suddenly increased from 23°.5 to 25°.8 C. (74°.3 to
78°.4 F.)

The geognostic constitution of the small islands
that surround the Isle of Pines was the more interesting to me, from the fact that I was slow to believe
the accounts of the coral structures of Polynesia,
that were said to rise from the profound depths of
the ocean to the surface of the water ; for it seemed to

me more probable that those enormous masses were founded upon some primitive or volcanic rock, to which they were attached at a small depth. The limestone formation of Güînes, partly compact and lithographic, and partly spongy, continued to Bataban6. It is very similar to the limestone formation of the Jura, and if we may judge simply by the external appearance, the Cayman islands are composed of the same rock. If the mountains of the Isle of Pines which present, according to the early historians of the conquest, the pine and palm together, are visible at a distance of twenty leagues, their height must be more than 3,200 feet; and I have been assured that they are composed also of a limestone similar to that of Güines.

From these facts, I expected to find the same rock (jurassic) in the Jardinillos; but I have only found, on examining the cays, which rise usually five or six inches above the surface of the water, a fragmentary rock in which regular lumps of coral are cemented, together with a quartz sand. Sometimes the fragments had a volume of one or two cubic feet, and the grains of sand have so completely disappeared, that one might believe that the lithophite polypus had remained there in numerous layers. The mass of this group of cays appeared to me to be a true agglomerate limestone, quite analogous to the tertiary limestone of the peninsula of Araya, near Cumaná, but of a more recent formation. The inequalities of these coral rocks, are filled with the detritus of shells and madrepore. All that rises above the surface of the sea is composed of broken lumps cemented by carbonate of lime, in which grains of quartz sands are held. I do not know if, under this fragmentary coral rock, structures of living polypus are to be found, at a great depth, and whether they adhere to the Jurassic formation.

Mariners believe that the sea gradually diminishes in depth in this vicinity, perhaps because they perceive the cays to grow and rise up, either from the sandbanks which the beating of the waves forms, or by successive agglutinations. Besides, it might not be impossible, that the widening of the Bahama channel, through which the waters of the Gulf Stream emerge, should cause in the lapse of time, a slight lowering of the level of the sea on the south side of Cuba, and particularly of the Gulf of Mexico, the centre of the great whirlpool of that pelagian river which washes the shores of the United States, and casts the fruits of tropical plants on the coasts of Norway.

The form of the coasts, the direction, force, and duration of certain currents, and certain winds, and the variations they experience from the changeable nature of the forces affecting them, are causes the concurrence of which for a long time within narrow and shallow limits might alter the equilibrium of the sea.[1] When the shores are so low that the level of the country for a league inland, varies only a few inches, these risings and fallings of the sea excite the imaginations of the inhabitants.

Cay Bonito (Beautiful Cay), which was the first I visited, is worthy of its name from the force of its vegetation. Everything indicates that it has been a long time above the surface of the ocean, for the interior of the cay is hardly lower than its margin. From a layer of sand and broken shells, covering the fragmentary coral rock to the depth of five or six inches, a forest of mangroves rises, which when seen from a distance, seem from their height and foliage to be laurel trees. The avicennia nitida, batis, small euphorbia, and several grassy plants, serve to fix the movable sand with their roots. But what particularly characterizes the flora of these

---

[1] I do not pretend to explain, by these same causes, the phenomena which we see on the coast of Sweden, where the sea has the appearance of an unequal fall at several points, amounting to from three to five feet in the century. A supposed analogy has occurred to the inhabitants of Dutch Guiana.—*Bolingbroke, Voyage to Demarara,* p. 148.—H.

coral islands[1] is the beautiful silver-leaved tourne-fortia gnaphalioides of Jacquin, which I first found there. It is not a solitary plant, and forms a tree four or five feet in height, its flowers having an agreeable odor. It also adorns Cay Flamenco, Cay de Piedras, and perhaps the greater part of the low islands of the Jardinillos.

While we were engaged in botanizing our sailors sought for sea crabs, and irritated with ill success, they soothed their anger by climbing the mangrove trees, and committing terrible havoc among the young *alcatraces*, which were snugly ensconced in pairs in the nests. Throughout Spanish America, this name is applied to the blackish, swan-sized peli-can of Buffon. The *alcatraz*, with that indolence and stupid confidence which characterizes the larger sea birds, forms its nest by twining together a few

[1] We gathered : Cenchrus myosuroides, Euphorbia buxifolia, Batis maritima, Iresine obtusifolia, Tournefortia gnaphalioides, Diomedea glabrata, Cakile cubensis, Dolichos miniatus, Parthenium hystero-phorus, etc. This latter plant, which we found in the valley of Caraccas, and on the temperate plains of Mexico, between elevations of three thousand and six thousand feet, grows in all the fields of Cuba. The inhabitants use it for aromatic baths, and to destroy fleas, which so abound within the tropics. In Cumaná many species of Casia are used, for their odor, against these troub'r insects.—H.

twigs only, and we often found four or five of these
in one tree. The young birds defended.themselves
valiantly with their bills, which were already six or
seven inches long, while the old ones flew above our
heads uttering hoarse and mournful cries; but the
streams of blood continued to trickle down the trees,
for the sailors were armed with clubs and cutlasses.
.Though we expostulated with them against this
cruelty and useless tormenting, they would not
desist; these men, accustomed to long obedience in
the solitude of the sea, take a singular pleasure in
exercising a cruel dominion over the animal creation whenever an opportunity presents itself. The
ground was covered with wounded birds, struggling
with death, so that this retired spot, which before
our arrival was the abode of peace, seemed now to
exclaim, Man has entered here.

The sky was covered with a reddish vapor, which
began to dissipate in the southwest, and we entertained the disappointed hope of seeing the Isle of
Pines. These regions possess a charm that is want-
·ing in the greater part of the New World, for they
recall to the mind memories which cluster round the
greatest names of the Spanish monarchy : Columbus
and Hernan Cortés. It was on the southern coast
of the island of Cuba, between the Bay of Jagua and
the Isle of Pines, that Columbus, during his second

voyage, beheld with admiration "that mysterious king who communicated with his subjects by signs only, and that group of men wearing long white gowns, like begging friars, while all the rest of the people were naked."

On his fourth voyage he met at the Jardinillos, the pirogues of the Mexican Indians, laden with the rich products and merchandise of Yucatan. Deceived by his ardent imagination, he seemed to hear from the lips of these navigators, "that they had come from a land where men rode upon horses, and wore crowns of gold upon their heads." "Already Cathay, the empire of the Gran Khan, and the mouths of the Ganges," seemed to be near to him, and he hoped soon to avail himself of the two Arabian interpreters, which he had taken on board at Cadiz when departing for America.[1]

---

[1] Compare *Lettera rarissima di Christoforo Colombo di 7 di Julio*, 1503, p. 2, with *Herrera, Dec.* 1, pp. 125–131. Nothing can be more tender or more pathetic, than the sorrowful tone that pervades this letter of Columbus, written at Jamaica, to the Catholic monarchs Ferdinand and Isabel. I particularly recommend to all who wish to study the character of that extraordinary man, his narrative of the nocturnal vision, when, in the midst of the tempest, a celestial voice soothed and cheered him with these words: "God made thy name to resound marvellously throughout the earth. The Indies, which is the richest portion of the earth, He has given thee for thine; thou hast divided it as thou wouldst, and He gave thee

Other memories that hover round the isle of Pines, belong to the conquest of Mexico. When Hernan Cortés was collecting his great expedition, his ship, the Capitana, grounded on one of the reefs of the Jardinillos, while sailing from the port of Trinidad for Cape San Antonio. For five days she was supposed to be lost, when the brave Pedro de Alvarado sent (in November, 1518) from the port of Carenas[1] (Havana) three vessels to his assis-

power so to do. To the boundaries of the ocean, that were closed with a mighty chain, He gave thee the key," etc. These lines, so full of sublime sentiment and poetry, have reached us only by an ancient Italian translation, for the Spanish original, cited in the "Nautical Biblioteca" of Don Antonio Leon, has not yet been found. We may add other expressions, full of candor, from the lips of him who discovered the New World. "Your highness may believe me," he said, "the globe of the world is not, by very much, so large as the vulgar suppose." On the same occasion, he says, "Seven years did I remain at your court, and during all that time I was told that my scheme was madness itself. Now, when I have opened the way, even tailors and shoemakers ask for grants to go and discover new lands. Persecuted and forgotten as I am, I never think upon Española and Paria, but my eyes fill with tears. Twenty years have I been in the service of your highness, and all my locks have whitened, my body has become weak, and now I cannot weep; weep for this, heaven, and weep for me, earth; weep for me who- ever has charity, truth, justice."—*Lett. rar.* pp. 13, 19, 34, 37.—H. The reader will find this letter, in Spanish, in Navarrete's "*Cole- cion de Viages,*" &c., vol. 1, page 299 *et sequiter.*

[1] At that time there were two settlements, one at the port of

tance. Subsequently, in February, 1519, Cortés
gathered his fleet near Cape San Antonio, probably
at the place which still bears the name of Bay of
Cortés, west of Bataban6, and opposite the Isle of
Pines. From that place, where he could more
easily free himself from the trammels which the
governor, Velasquez, was preparing to throw around
him, he sailed, almost clandestinely, for the shores
of Mexico. Strange vicissitudes of human affairs!
A handful of men, landing from the extreme west
of Cuba upon the coast of Yucatan, tore down the
empire of Montezuma; and in our time, three centuries later, this same Yucatan, which is part of the confederation of independent Mexican States, has almost
menaced a conquest of the western shores of Cuba.[1]

Carenas, in the ancient Indian province of Habana (Herrera, Dec.
1, pp. 276–277), and another, the greatest, at the city of San Cristobal de Cuba. In 1519 the two settlements were united, and the port
of Carenas took the name of San Cristobal de la Habana. "Cortés,"
says Herrera (Dec. 11, pp. 80 and 95), "went to the village of San
Cristobal, which, at that time, was on the south coast, and afterwards
went to Havana."—H.

[1] Humboldt, probably, alludes here to the secret society of "The
Black Eagle," which had its principal centre in Mexico, but
extended its ramifications throughout Cuba, its object being to
achieve the independence of that island. It was discovered and
suppressed about the time of his writing, 1825, when its plans had
very nearly reached maturity, and many eminent Cubans were
forced to flee their country.

On the 11th of March, we visited Cay Flamenco. I found its latitude to be 21° 59′ 39″. The centre of the island is low, rising only fourteen inches above the level of the sea. The water on it is brackish, while that on the other cays is perfectly fresh. The mariners of Cuba, as well as the inhabitants of the lagoons of Venice, and some modern physiologists, attribute this absence of salt to the action of the sand as the water filters through it. But how is this action exerted, where its supposed existence is not justified by any chemical analogy? Besides, these cays are composed of rocks, and not of sand; and their small extent presents an objection to the supposition that it is rain water which has gathered and remains standing. Perhaps the fresh water on the cays flows from the adjacent coast, or even from the mountains of Cuba, by the effect of hydrostatic pressure. This would prove that the strata of Jurassic limestone extends under the sea, and that the coral rock is superposed on the limestone.[1]

The belief that every spring of fresh or salt water

[1] The ancients were acquainted with these eruptions of fresh water in the sea, near Bayas, Syracuse, and Arado (Phœnicia). The coral islands that surround Radak, particularly the very low island of Otdia, also contain fresh water. A careful examination of these phenomena at the level of the sea, cannot be too strongly recommended to travellers.—H.

is a local phenomenon, is an error that is too widely
disseminated, for currents of water circulate in the
interior of the earth for long distances, between
strata of peculiar density or nature, as do the rivers
that wear the surface of the globe.   Don Francisco
Lemaur, the learned engineer, who subsequently displayed such energy and valor in the defence of the
castle of San Juan de Ulua, informed me that in the
bay of Jagua, half a degree east of the Jardinillos,
springs of fresh water are found boiling up in the
midst of the sea, two and a half leagues from the
shore.[1] The water rushes from these springs with
sufficient force to cause a dashing of the waves,
making the vicinity dangerous for small canoes.
Vessels that do not wish to go into the harbor of
Jagua, sometimes fill their casks at these sea fountains, and the water is more or less cold according as
they take it near to, or far from the bottom.   The
Manatees (sea calves), guided by their instinct, have
discovered this region of fresh water, and the fishermen, who are very fond of the flesh of these *cetaceos*

---

[1] Similar springs of fresh water occur in the bay of Cardenas, on
the north coast of Cuba, springing forth with such strength that
fresh water can be dipped up with a bucket, in the midst of the sea
water. We have been told that in some parts of that town, running
water is found under the earth, on sinking wells a short distance.

herbivoros, find them there in abundance, and kill them in the open sea.[1]

About half a mile from Cay Flamenco, we sailed near two rocks level with the sea, against which the

---

[1] The following is Dampier's clear description of this animal, which is still found in some places on the south side of Cuba: "This creature is about the bigness of a horse, and ten or twelve feet long. The mouth of it is much like the mouth of a cow, having great, thick lips. The eyes are no bigger than a small pea; the ears are only two small holes in the side of the head. The neck is short and thick, bigger than the head. The biggest part of this creature is at the shoulders, where it hath two large fins on each side of its belly. Under each of these fins the female hath a small dug to suckle its young. From the shoulders, towards its tail, it retains its bigness for about a foot, then groweth smaller and smaller to the very tail, which is flat, and about fourteen inches broad, and twenty inches long, and the middle four or five inches thick, but about the edges it is not above two inches thick. From the head to the tail it is round and smooth, without any fin but those two before mentioned. I have heard that some weigh twelve hundred pounds, but I never saw any so large. The Manatee delights to live in brackish water, and they are commonly in creeks and rivers near the sea. * * * They live on grass seven or eight inches long, which grows in the sea in many places. They never come on shore, nor into shallow water where they cannot swim. Their flesh is white, both the fat and the lean, and extraordinary sweet, wholesome meat. The skin of the bull, or of the back of the cow, is very thick, and of it they make horsewhips. While the thongs are green, they twist them, and hang them to dry, which, in a week's time, become as hard as wood."— *Voyas Round the World*, vol. 1, p. 38.

waves dash loudly. They were the Piedras de Diego Perez. The temperature of the sea, at the surface, fell there to 22°.6 C. (72°.7 F.), the depth of water being only six and a half feet. In the afternoon, we reached Cay de Piedras, which. is formed by two rocks with breakers between, running N.N.E. and W.S.W. As these two rocks are some distance apart (forming the eastern side of the Jardinillos), many vessels are lost upon them. The cay has hardly any trees upon it, for those who are shipwrecked there, have cut them down in their need to make signal fires. The shore is very steep toward the sea, but near the middle there is a small channel with still water.

We found inclosed in the rock a lump of madrepore, more than three cubic feet in size; and we entertained no doubt that the limestone formation, which from a distance appears much like the Jurassic limestone, was a fragmentary rock. It is desirable that geognostic travellers should some day examine the entire chain of cays that surround the island of Cuba, in order to determine what is due to the insects that still labor in the depths of the sea, and what belongs to the true tertiary formations, whose epoch approaches very nearly with that of the coarse limestone which abounds among the remains of the coral lithophites. That which generally rises

above the sea is usually nothing more than a species
of marble, or a collection of fragments of madrepore,
cemented by carbonate of lime, with broken shells
and sand.   It is important to examine, in each cay,
upon what this class of rock rests; if it rises from
works of still living mollusca, or from those secondary and tertiary rocks, which, from the appearance
and preservation of the coral remains they contain,
might be supposed to be modern productions.   The
gypsum of the cays off San Juan de los Remedios,
on the northern coast of Cuba, is worthy of great
attention; for its epoch surely ascends beyond the
era of history, and no geognostic observer will deem
it to be the product of the mollusca of our seas.

It was from Cay de Piedras that we first saw,
toward the east-northeast, the high mountains that
rise back of the bay of Jagua.   We again passed
the night at anchor, and on the following morning,
the 12th of March, running out between the north
point of Cay de Piedras and the coast of Cuba, we
entered upon the clear and open sea.   Its deep blue
color, and increased temperature, proved to us the
much greater depth of the water.   The thermometer,
which, in soundings of six and a half, and eight feet
of water, we had often found at 22°.6 C. (72°.7 F.),
now rose to 26°.2 C. (79° F.), while during these
observations it stood in the air at from 25° to 27° C.
(77° to 80°.6 F.).   Availing ourselves of the varia-

tions of the land and sea breezes, we kept to the eastward as far as the port of Trinidad, in order to take advantage during our voyage to Carthagena, of the constant northeast winds which then prevailed.

Passing the marshy coast of Camareos, where Bartolome de las Casas, so celebrated for his humanity and noble valor, obtained in 1514, from his friend Velasquez the governor, a good assignment of Indians,[1] we arrived off the bay of Jagua. This harbor is one of the most excellent, and at the same time least frequented in the island. "There may not be another like it in the world," said the old chronicler, Antonio de Herrera; and the surveys and plans for its defence, made by Señor Lemaur, under commission from the Count de Jaruco, have demonstrated that the haven of Jagua is worthy of the celebrity it has obtained from the times of the conquest. A hamlet and a small castle is all that is yet found there, but they serve to prevent the English from careening their ships in the harbor, as they did, without concern, during the war with Spain.[2]

---

[1] He renounced it in the same year during a short stay in Jamaica, from conscientious scruples.—H.

[2] The flourishing town of Cienfuegos now stands upon the borders of this fine harbor, which is the scene of an active commerce at the present time, and the germ of rich promise for the future.

East of Jagua the hills of San Juan approach the coast, and present a very majestic appearance, not so much from their height, which does not exceed 1,900 feet,[1] as from their steep declivities and general form. I was told that the shore, as far as the mouth of the Guaurabo river, is so bold and steep that a ship may lie alongside it at any point. In the evening, when the temperature of the sea fell to 23° C. (73°.4 F.), and the breeze came from the land, we perceived that delightful fragrance of flowers and honey, so characteristic of the shores of Cuba.[2] We sailed along the coast, at a distance of two or three miles, and just before sunset, on the 13th of March, we found ourselves off the mouth of the river San Juan, so much feared by mariners because

[1] Estimated distance three marine leagues. Angle of altitude, not corrected for the curve of the earth and refraction, 1° 47' 10". Height, 1745 feet.—H.

[2] I have already observed that the wax of Cuba, which is an important article in its commerce, is due to the bees of Europe (of the genus Apis, Latr.). Columbus expressly says, that in his time the natives of Cuba did not gather wax. The great cake of this substance, which he found in the island on his first voyage, and which was presented to King Ferdinand, in the celebrated audience at Barcelona, was found afterwards, to have been brought by Mexican pirogues from Yucatan. It is curious to observe that the wax of the *Melipones* was the first Mexican production that fell into the hands of the Spaniards, in the month of November, 1492.—H.

of the innumerable mosquitoes and sand-flies that fill the air.

The mouth of the river looks like the break of a deep ravine, in which large vessels might enter, were it not for a shoal that closes the channel. This port is much frequented by smugglers from Jamaica, and even by pirates from New Providence. The hills which rise back of it have a height of about 1,450 feet. I passed a great portion of the night upon deck. What lonely shores are these, where not even the light of a fisherman's hut is to be seen! From Batabanó to Trinidad, a distance of fifty leagues, there is not a single village, and only two or three farms where swine and cattle are reared; yet in the time of Columbus, that land was inhabited along its whole extent of shore. When wells are dug here, and when torrents of water, during the heavy rains, wash the surface of the earth, stone hatchets and a few copper utensils[1] are found, the only remains of the ancient inhabitants of the place.

[1] Doubtless, from the copper of Cuba, for the abundance of this metal, in a native state, must have stimulated the Indians of Cuba and Hayti to smelt it. Columbus states, " that in Hayti, masses of native copper of one hundred and fifty pounds weight were found, and that the pirogues of Yucatan, which he met on the south coast of Cuba, carried among other Mexican merchandise, crucibles for smelting copper."—*Herrera, Dec.* 1, pp. 86 & 131.—H.

At sunrise, I persuaded our captain to sound, and at sixty fathoms we did not reach bottom. The temperature of the surface water was much warmer than we had found it elsewhere, being 26°.8 C., (80° F.), exceeding by 4°.2 C. our observations near the breakers of Diego Perez. Half a mile from the shore, the water was only 25°.5 C., (78° F.), and although we had no opportunity to sound, I do not doubt that the depth was less. On the 14th of March, we entered the river Guaurabo, one of the ports of Trinidad, to land the Batabanó pilot who had run us on the mud so often while crossing the banks of the Jardinillos. We also hoped to find there a mail packet, under whose convoy we might sail to Carthagena. I landed in the afternoon, and set on the beach Bordas' dip-needle, and an artificial horizon, in order to observe the passage of several stars across the meridian; but we had hardly begun our preparations, when some Catalan shop-keepers, who had been dining on board a foreign vessel which had lately arrived, invited us with many demonstrations of pleasure to accompany them to the city. These honest people made us mount, two on each horse, and as the heat was excessive we did not hesitate to accept their frank and simple offer.

Trinidad is four miles from the mouth of the Guaurabo in a northeast direction, and the road runs through a plain apparently formed by long-standing water. It is covered with a beautiful vegetation, to which the *Miraguama*, a species of palm with shining leaves, which we there saw for the first time, gives a peculiar character. This fertile land, although of the red soil, only waits the hand of man to clear and cultivate it, when it will yield abundant crops. Toward the west there is a picturesque view of the hills of San Juan, which form a limestone chain very steep on its southern side, and some 1,800 or 2,000 feet high, their naked and arid summits now rounded and now forming high and steep peaks.[1]

Though the temperature falls very low here during the season of the northers it never snows, but frost and hail only are sometimes seen in these mountains, and in those of St. Jago. I have spoken elsewhere of the difficulty of explaining this absence. On leaving the woods a curtain of hills is seen, the southern slope of which is covered with houses. This is the city of Trinidad, founded by Diego Velasquez in 1514, stimulated thereto by the rich gold mines said to have been discovered in the little

---

[1] Wherever the rock is seen, I have found a compact whitish-brown limestone, in part porous, and in part with smooth fracture, like the Jurassic formation.—H.

valley of the Arimao river.[1] All the streets of
Trinidad are very steep, and the inhabitants there
complain, as they also do in the greater part of
Spanish America, of the bad selection made by the
conquerors of sites for the towns they founded.[2]
The church of Nuestra Señora de la Popa, a celebrated place for pic-nics, stands on the northern side of
the town.

Its site appeared to me to be about seven hundred
feet above the level of the sea, and commands, as do
also the greater part of the streets in the town, a
magnificent view of the ocean, the two ports,
Casilda and Guaurabo, a forest of palms, and the high
group of the hills of San Juan. As I had forgotten
to bring the barometer and other instruments to the
city, I endeavored on the following morning to
ascertain the height of the hill on which the church
stands, by taking alternate altitudes of the sun above

[1] This river empties into the bay of Jagua, on its eastern side.—H.

[2] May not the city begun by Velasquez, have, perhaps, been
founded in the plain, nearer to the ports of Casilda and Guaurabo?
Many of the inhabitants suppose that the fear of the French,
Portuguese, and English pirates (*flibustiers*), induced the selection
of an inland site upon the sides of the hills, from whence, as from a
high tower, the approach of the enemy might be discovered; but it
seems to me that these fears could not have existed before the time
of Hernando de Soto (1538). The city of Havana was first sacked
by the French corsairs, in 1539.—H.

the horizon of the sea, and above an artificial horizon. I had practised this method at the castle of
Murviedro, the ruins of Saguntum, and Cape Blanco
near La Guaira: but the sea horizon was clouded,
and broken in several places by dark streaks, which
indicated the existence of small currents of air, or a
series of extraordinary refractions.[1]

We were entertained in Trinidad at the house of
Señor Muñoz, the collector of customs, with a charming hospitality. I continued my observations during
the greater part of the night under rather unfavor-
able circumstances, and found the latitude near the
cathedral to be 21° 48' 20". My chronometrical longi-
tude was 82° 21' 7". I learned on my second visit
to Havana, on my return from Mexico, that this longi-
tude was very nearly the same with that observed by
Captain José del Rio, who long resided there, and
also that that officer placed the latitude of the city
in 21° 42' 40". I have discussed this disagreement
in another work, and it will suffice to note here that
Mon. Puysegur found the latitude to be 21° 47' 15",

[1] In the opinion of the great naturalist, Wollaston, whom I had the
pleasure of consulting relative to this curious phenomenon, these black
streaks consist, probably, of that portion of the atmosphere nearest
to the surface of the ocean when the wind begins to ruffle it. In
this case, the true horizon, which was more distant, would be made
invisible to the eye by the opposition of color.—H.

and that observations of four stars in the Great Bear, made by Gamboa, gave to Mon. Oltmanns while ascertaining the declination according to Piazzi's catalogue, a latitude of 21° 46′ 25."

The lieutenant governor of Trinidad, whose jurisdiction then comprised Villa Clara, Santi Espiritu, and Puerto Principe, was a nephew of the celebrated astronomer, Don Antonio Ulloa. He gave us a great dinner at which we met several of the French refugees from St. Domingo, who had brought hither only their industry and their intellectual acquirements. The export of sugar from Trinidad, according to the returns made up at Havana, did not then exceed four thousand boxes. The inhabitants complained of the impediments which the general government, in its unjust preference for Havana, placed in the way of the agricultural and commercial development of the Central and Eastern districts of the island; as also of the great accumulation of wealth, population, and authority at the capital, while the rest of the country was almost a wilderness. Many minor centres, distributed at regular distances through the island, were preferred to the prevailing system, which had resulted in attracting to a single point, wealth, corruption of manners, and the yellow fever. Similar exaggerated accusations, and complaints of provincial cities against the capi-

tal, occur in all countries. It cannot be doubted
that in political organizations, as in physical, the
general welfare depends upon the uniform distribution of the partial life; but we must distinguish
between the preëminence which flows from the
natural course of things, and that which results from
the policy and acts of the government.

Discussions have often arisen at Trinidad, as to
which of the two ports is the best; and perhaps it
would be better if the municipal council should
endeavor to improve either one of them with the
small amount of means at its command. The distance of the city from Casilda, and from the mouth
of the Guaurabo, is. very nearly the same, but the
cost of transportation of goods is greatest to the
former.[1] The mouth of the Guaurabo, defended by
a newly erected battery, has a safe anchorage, but it
is not so well sheltered as that of Casilda.

Vessels of light draught can ascend the river to
within a mile of the city. The mail packets to Costa
Firme generally prefer the Guaurabo, as they can
enter it safely without a pilot.

The port of Casilda is more enclosed by the land,
but cannot be entered without a local pilot, because

[1] A railroad now runs from the city to Casilda, which has been
much improved.

of the Mulas and Mulatto reefs. The great wharf which was built of wood, and was formerly very useful to commerce, was injured while landing some large pieces of artillery, and is now entirely destroyed; doubtless it would be better to rebuild it of stone, as proposed by Don Luis de Bassecourt, or to deepen the bar of the Guaurabo by dredging. The great fault of the port of Casilda, is the want of fresh water, which shipping must procure on the other side of its western point, exposing them to capture by privateers in time of war. We were assured that the population of Trinidad, and the plantations around it within a radius of one league, amounted to nineteen thousand souls. The cultivation of sugar and coffee has increased greatly, but the cereals of Europe are grown only further north toward Villa Clara.

We passed the evening very agreeably at the residence of Don Antonio Padron, one of the most wealthy inhabitants, where we met nearly all the principal residents of Trinidad. We again were surprised, as we had been at the capital, with the mirthfulness and quick intelligence of the Cuban ladies. These are happy, natural gifts, which the refinement of European civilization may make more attractive, but which are extremely pleasing in their primitive simplicity.

17*

On the evening of the 15th of March, we left
Trinidad, and our departure was widely different
from our arrival, on horseback with the Catalan
shopkeepers. The municipal council sent us to the
mouth of the Guaurabo in a coach lined with ancient
red damask; and to increase the embarrassment we
felt, an ecclesiastic, who was also the poet of the
place, dressed throughout in velvet notwithstanding
the great heat, celebrated in a sonnet our voyage to
the Orinoco. On the way to the harbor we were sin-
gularly surprised with a spectacle which a residence
of more than two years in the tropics should have
made familiar to us.

Nowhere else have I seen such an innumerable
quantity of fireflies [1] (*coouyos*), for trees, branches,
and leaves glowed with them in their brilliant and
moving light, the intensity of which varies with the
will of the insect that produces it; it seemed to me
as though the starry vault of heaven had fallen
upon the plain. In the habitations of the poorer
classes in the county, a dozen of these insects placed
in a perforated gourd, suffice for a light during the
night. By shaking the gourd quickly, the insect is
roused, and lights up the luminous discs which are
placed on each side of its head. The inhabitants

[1] Elater noctilucus.—H.

employ a truthful and simple. expression, in saying
that a gourd filled with cocuyos is an ever-lighted
torch; and in fact it is only extinguished by the
death of the insects which are easily kept alive
with a little sugar cane. A lady in Trinidad told
us that during a long and painful passage from
Costa Firme, she had availed herself of these phos-
phorescent insects whenever she wished to give the
breast to her child at night. The captain of the
ship would not permit any other light on board at
night, for fear of the privateers.

As the breeze continued to freshen, and haul
steadily to the northeast, we laid our course so as to
clear the Cayman islands, but the current swept us
toward them. Steering south quarter east, we soon
lost sight of the palm-covered shore, of the hills
that rise over Trinidad, and finally of the high
mountains of Cuba. There is something impressive
in the contemplation of a land which one is leaving,
as it sinks, steadily and slowly beneath the horizon
of the sea. This impression was increased to us, in
its interest and grave import, at this time, when St:
Domingo, then the centre of great political agita-
tion, threatened to involve the surrounding islands in
one of those bloody struggles which demonstrate to
man the ferocity of his nature. Happily these
fears and-menaces were not realized, for the tempest

lulled in the land that gave it birth, and a free black
population, instead of disturbing the repose of the
neighboring islands, has made some progress towards
a suavity of manners, and the establishment of good
civil institutions.[1]

Haiti is surrounded by Cuba, Porto Rico, and
Jamaica, with a population of 370,000 white and
885,000 blacks, while she contains 900,000 blacks
and mulattoes, who have freed themselves by their
own will, and the good fortune of their arms. These
negroes, engaged much more in the cultivation of
alimenticious plants than of colonial staples, increase
with a rapidity that is exceeded only by the population of the United States. Will the tranquillity
which the Spanish and English islands have enjoyed,
during the twenty-six years that have passed since

[1] How sad to contemplate, in the present debased condition of the
Haitian blacks, the failure of these noble and humane hopes. Yet
the erroneous social theories upon which they are based, have been
extended by the governments of Europe over many of the islands
of the Antilles, and Cuba, and Porto Rico alone remain, unab-
sorbed in the black abyss of barbarism, whose waves have rolled
over the other West Indian isles, extinguishing the lights of
their civilization, and the hopes of their humanity. We may here
read the instructive lesson, that the principles upon which a social
organism is based, cannot be violently changed without destroying
its vital principle, and bringing desolation and death to the tempo-
ral and spiritual interests of its members.

the first revolution in Haiti, continue to inspire the whites with that fatal security, which disdainfully resists any improvement in the state of the servile class? On every side of that Mediterranean of the Antilles, on the west and on the south, in Mexico, in Guatemala, and in Colombia, the new legislators are laboring with zeal to extinguish slavery; and it may be hoped that the union of these imperious circumstances will assist the beneficent intentions of the several European governments, who wish to improve continually the condition of the slaves; for the fear of danger will force those concessions which the eternal principles of justice and humanity demand.

THE END.

J. C. DERBY'S

RECENT PUBLICATIONS.

THE WIDOW BEDOTT PAPERS: Containing, also, the Experiences of Aunt
    Maguire. Edited by ALICE B. NEAL. With eight humorous illustrations by
    Dallas and Orr. 12mo. $1 25

MARRIED, NOT MATED. A Novel. By ALICE CAREY, ... 1 25

WINNIE AND I. A Novel. 12mo. 1 00

ISORA'S CHILD. A Novel. 12mo. 1 25

CAMP FIRES OF THE RED MEN. By J. R. ORTON, M.D. 12mo. Illustrated, . 1 25

PEN PICTURES OF THE BIBLE. By CHARLES BEECHER. First Series: David
    and his Throne. Uniform with "Sunny Side," 50

COUNTRY MARGINS, AND SUMMER RAMBLES. By HAMMOND and MANSFIELD, 1 00

SIMM'S LIFE OF GENERAL MARION. 12mo. Illustrated, ... 1 25

LIVES OF THE SIGNERS OF THE DECLARATION OF INDEPENDENCE.
    Illustrated. 12mo., ... 1 25

LAYARD'S POPULAR DISCOVERIES AT NINEVEH. 12mo. Illustrations, . 1 00

HOWE'S EMINENT MECHANICS. 12mo. Illustrated, ... 1 25

STEPHENS' INCIDENTS OF TRAVEL IN EGYPT AND THE HOLY LAND. A
    new edition. 8vo. Illustrated, ... 2 00

    THE SAME, 2 vols., 12mo., ... 2 00

HANNAH MORE'S COMPLETE WORKS. 2 vols., ... 8 00

PILGRIM'S PROGRESS. A fine edition, with fifty elegant engravings. 12mo., . 75

MISS SEDGWICK'S WORKS. 8 vols., viz.:

    REDWOOD. 12mo., ... 1 25

    CLARENCE. " 1 25

    A NEW ENGLAND TALE. 12mo., ... 1 25

MRS. TUTHILL'S SUCCESS IN LIFE. 4 vols., 12mo., viz. :

 THE MECHANIC, ... 68

 THE MERCHANT, ... 68

 THE LAWYER, ... 68

 THE ARTIST, ... 68

LANE'S BRIGADE IN MEXICO, ... 75

BARNARD'S SCHOOL ARCHITECTURE. 8vo., ... 2 00

THE MYSTIC CIRCLE; OR, HAND-BOOK OF MASONRY, ... 1 50

TAYLOR'S HISTORY OF OHIO. 12mo., ... 1 50

ECLECTIC PRACTICE OF MEDICINE. By. Drs. Newton and Powell. 8vo., . 4 50

THE YOUNG WIFE. By Wm. A. Alcott, M.D., ... 1 00

THE YOUNG HUSBAND. By Wm. A. Alcott, M.D., ... 1 00

THE YOUNG MOTHER. By Wm. A. Alcott, M.D., ... 1 00

THE YOUNG HOUSEKEEPER. By Wm. A. Alcott, M.D., ... 1 00

THE HOUSE I LIVE IN. By Wm. A. Alcott, M.D., ... 68

INDIAN NARRATIVES. 18mo., ... 75

WEBSTER FAMILY CYCLOPÆDIA. 7000 Receipts, 100 Engravings, . . 3 00

ILLUSTRATED LIFE OF FRANKLIN. 8vo., ... 2 00

DON QUIXOTE. A new edition, cloth, 12mo., ... 1 25

GIL BLAS. A new edition, 12mo. 1 25

THE HEART OF MABEL WARE. A Novel. 12mo., . . 1 00

ROORBACH'S BOOKSELLERS' TRADE LIST,

Containing a Complete Catalogue of American Publications from 1820 to 1852. Price $5, net. Every Bookseller in the land should possess it. Not only is the name of each book given, but the Publisher and the Price. Well studied, it will make a complete Bookseller of the uninitiated.

LIST OF POPULAR BOOKS

FOR AGENTS.

FLORA'S INTERPRETER. Edited by Sarah J. Hale. 12mo.,	$1 25
GREEN MOUNTAIN BOYS. By D. P. Thompson. 12mo.,	1 00
THE RANGERS. By the Author of "Green Mountain Boys." 12mo.,	1 00
MAY MARTIN. By the same. 12mo.,	1 00
COMBE ON THE CONSTITUTION OF MAN. 12mo.,	75
MECHANIC'S OWN BOOK. 12mo.,	1 00
ETHAN ALLEN; or, The Green Mountain Heroes. 12mo.,	1 25
UPS AND DOWNS; or, Silver Lake Sketches. By Cousin Cicely. 12mo.,	1 25
LEWIE; or, The Bended Twig. By Same,	1 00
ALONE. By the Author of "Hidden Path." 12mo.,	1 25
WESTERN SCENES AND ADVENTURES. 12mo.,	1 25
SALT WATER BUBBLES; or, Life on the Wave. 12mo.,	1 25
HALL'S LEGENDS OF THE WEST. 12mo.,	1 25
THE WIDE WIDE WORLD. By Elizabeth Wetherell. 2 vols.,	1 50
QUEECHY. By the author of "Wide Wide World." 2 vols.,	1 75
MR. RUTHERFORD'S CHILDREN. 16mo., By the Same,	75
HUMANITY IN THE CITY. By Rev. E. H. Chapin. 12mo.,	1 00
MRS. SIGOURNEY'S SELECT POEMS. 12mo.,	1 25
MRS. SIGOURNEY'S SAYINGS FOR THE LITTLE ONES. 16mo.,	75
D'AUBIGNÉ'S HISTORY OF PROTESTANTS. 12mo.,	1 25
FERN LEAVES. By Fanny Fern. First Series,	1 25
Do. do. do. do. Second Series,	1 25
HOME SCENES AND HOME SOUNDS. By Mrs. Stephens,	1 00
LITTLE CROSS BEARERS. By Miss Chesebro',	50
THE WORKS OF FLAVIUS JOSEPHUS. 8vo.,	1 25
FAMILY QUARTO BIBLE. Plain sheep,	2 00
Do. do. do. A. P. C. marble edges,	3 50
Do. do. do. A. P. C. gilt edges,	5 00

44

TWO NEW BOOKS BY PETER PARLEY!

THE BALLOON TRAVELS OF ROBERT MERRY

AND HIS YOUNG FRIENDS OVER VARIOUS COUNTRIES OF EUROPE.

Edited by PETER PARLEY.

With 8 Original Designs. Beautiful 12mo. $1 00.

THE
VOYAGES, TRAVELS, AND ADVENTURES

OF GILBERT GO-AHEAD, IN FOREIGN PARTS.

Edited by PETER PARLEY.

With 8 Original Designs. Beautiful 12mo. $1 00.

ALSO, NEARLY READY,

GREEN MOUNTAIN GIRLS,

A TALE OF VERMONT.

One neat 12mo. Price $1 00.

THE LOST HUNTER,

A TALE OF EARLY TIMES.

12mo., $1 25.

THE CREOLE ORPHANS,

A TALE OF LOUISIANA.

12mo., $1 25.

TWO STANDARD HISTORIES FOR EVERY LIBRARY.

GILLIES' HISTORY OF GREECE,

ITS COLONIES AND CONQUESTS, TO THE DIVISION OF THE MACEDONIAN EMPIRE.

Including the History of Literature, Philosophy, and the Fine Arts.

Complete in one volume. Illustrated, 8vo. $1 75.

FERGUSON'S HISTORY OF ROME.

THE HISTORY OF THE PROGRESS AND TERMINATION OF THE ROMAN REPUBLIC.

With a Notice of the Author, by Lord JEFFREY.

Uniform with Gillies' History of Greece. $1 75.

THE AMERICAN GIFT BOOK;

A PERPETUAL SOUVENIR.

With Six elegant Steel Engravings, viz.: "The Marriage of Washington," "Goddess of Liberty," "Portrait of Washington," "Portrait of Daniel Webster," "Spirit of '76," "Portrait of Martha Washington." Together with "Washington's Farewell Address," "Constitution of the United States," and the "Declaration of Independence." Price $1; cloth, full gilt, $1 50.

"The getting-up of this nice volume was a happy thought. It awakens and invigorates the noblest patriotic sentiments, and, withal, fortifies patriotism by Bible religion. The volume opens with 'Washington's Farewell Address,' among the richest legacies ever bestowed by a patriot upon his country; and then follows, in prose and poetry, the happiest and most soul-stirring appeals to the reason and hearts of Americans, warning them of the danger of foreign influence adverse to their free institutions, and exciting to sleepless vigilance in their perpetuation. The book gives a clear exhibition of what the Know-Nothings' are; shows the necessity for such an association; and excites an earnest hope that they may be preserved and prospered as the life-guard of civil and religious liberty."—*Christian Advocate and Journal.*

"This is a sterling annual, full of living truth which must be commended by every editor who is not a Jesuit at heart, and find a response in the soul of every lover of American soil and institutions. Every page in it is of sterling value, and should be committed to memory, and handed down from father to child. The matter in such a book is its own best adornment. Washington and the worthies following after him here speak in the living present, and poets of the soil set to glowing measure the glories of our Protestant birthright."—*Albany Spectator.*

"We venture to say that so far as the *contents* are concerned, this gift-book will not be excelled by any which will be issued this season. Besides these, there are nearly one hundred American articles of a truly American character, many of them written by the brightest stars in the splendid galaxy of American Authors."—*Christian Freeman.*

"We doubt if in any similar compass of modern literature so many fine thoughts, both in poetry and prose, can be found crowded together. The Webster Hulsemann letter is among the contributions, and some of the best poetry of our patriotic writers."—*N. Y. Express.*

"We earnestly commend this book, and because it is a good one—good for the times, for the people, and for the American cause. It cannot fail to become a favorite. Let the *Wide-Awake* be found before every American face and eye."—*Boston Bee.*

"The articles are all patriotic effusions, calculated to arouse the true American feeling. The K. N.'s will greet with delight the work, and peruse its pages with avidity and interest."—*Williamsburgh Times.*

"We predict an immense sale for the volume, which is so thoroughly American in subject and sentiment, and a product of American talent and genius that will be prized by all true Americans."—*Boston Transcript.*

A BOOK OF RARE BEAUTY AND GREAT INTEREST.

FOURTH EDITION NOW READY.

MRS. OAKES SMITH'S NEW ROMANCE.

BERTHA AND LILY:

OR, THE PARSONAGE OF BEECH GLEN:

1 elegant 12mo. vol. Price $1.

The following brief extracts are but the key-notes of lengthy reviews. No recent book has received more marked attention from the press:

" It compels the reader to linger over its pages."—*N. Y. Tribune.*

" Sparkling thoughts and humane and benevolent feelings."—*Albany Argus.*

" More powerfully written than any recent work of fiction."—*N. Y. Day Book.*

" Another story of exquisite beauty—graceful and fascinating."—*Phila. News.*

" Altogether it is a remarkable book."—*N. Y. Christian Enquirer.*

" No romance more deserves a wide-spread popularity."—*Providence Post.*

" Striking truths boldly represented."—*Rural New Yorker.*

" Springing from a heart overflowing with love and sympathy."—*Pittsburg Visiter.*

" Strange scenes, powerful dialogue, and exquisite imagery."—*Transcript.*

" We know of one woman who says it is a brave book."—*Boston Commonwealth.*

" Elegant with mountain and valley flowers and water lilies."—*N. Y. Dispatch.*

" Womanly genius under its happiest and purest inspirations."—*Albany Atlas.*

" A 'romance,' but full of life. It has power; it has truth."—*Boston Bee.*

" Sure to captivate the reader."—*N. Y. Atlas.*

" The ladies will find it a graceful and fascinating production."—*Phila. City Item.*

" Just what might be expected from a brilliant woman."—*Albany Express.*

" A female delicacy of taste and perception."—*Ladies' Repository.*

" A moral perspective of rare beauty and significance."—*Harpers' Magazine.*

" So intensely interesting, we read it at one sitting."—*Cleveland Farmer.*

" A 'prose poem,' replete with melody and imagery."—*Boston Chronicle.*

" Well vindicated her reputation as a woman of genius."—*N. Y. Herald.*

" True to nature and every day life."—*Albany Spectator.*

" Cannot fail to inspire the reader with noble purposes."—*Christian Freeman.*

" Will be eagerly sought for and read."—*Water Cure Journal.*

" The style is glowing and impassioned."—*Rochester American.*

" Its pages leave a very attractive impression."—*Salem Gazette.*

" Will prove a valuable accession to the home circle."—*Ladies' Enterprise.*

" Will be read, and find many enthusiastic readers."—*Bangor Mercury.*

" A beautiful creation."—*Boston Transcript.*

" Comes before the reader with freshness, earnestness and power."—*Eclectic.*

" The book before us is bravely written."—*Providence Una.*

" The very best fiction we have read for years."—*Glen's Fall Republican.*

" Characters in it worthy of lasting fame."—*Hartford Republican.*

" All her works bear the impress of genius."—*Olive Branch.*

" It is a beautiful story."—*Sandusky Democrat.*

THE WHITE DOVE, AND OTHER BALLADS FOR CHILDREN.

BY MRS. E. W. TOWNSEND,

OF PHILADELPHIA.

16mo., Illustrated.   Price, 50 cents; full gilt sides and edges, 75 cents.

"Dean Swift, or Sterne, or Doctor Johnson, or somebody else, when in doubt about the quality of any new literary effort, used to read it to the housekeeper. If she understood and liked it, no doubt it was true to nature. Adopting this plan, we called up a little boy and girl to try this book upon. The boy flung himself into a chair and put his leg over the arm, as if he expected to be bored. The small damsel took to the rug as for a nap. We tried the Snow Storm about Bruno and his children, with success highly flattering to the authoress. The small damsel sat up, pushed back her curls and opened her eyes very wide. The boy looked away off out of the window, and swung his cowhide boots about as if he didn't care. But the tears, not few nor small, glistened in the eyes of both, We think the book will do."— *Vermont Statesman.*

" Good rhymes for children are rare indeed, and this will make this elegant little volume a welcome addition to the juvenile library. The lady holds a graceful and familiar pen, and the children will know her poems only to love and remember them. Many a boy and girl will be happier for its cheerful pictures, pretty thoughts and good sentiments. A book like this is worth a hundred copies of ' Mother Goose ' or any of her family. Those who would form a taste for good reading in the young, should place such books as this in their hands."— *Worcester Palladium.*

" The sweetest and happiest productions in that class of writing that we have met with for a long time. The conceits are full of the finest and most delicate fancy, and the versification is music itself. The narratives are so simple and natural that childhood will comprehend and enjoy them, while the delicately-drawn pictures of life and nature possess a charm that may well beguile the hours of age."— *U. S. Magazine.*

" Here's a nice book for nice little people; full of poetry, pictures and beautiful stories, printed in large type, on fine white paper, and *bound* to be read. Children who love good books will be largely indebted to those who publish such excellent ones as The White Dove."— *Gospel Banner.*

" The writer has succeeded in clothing the purest sentiments in natural and touching verse. Love of nature, and sympathy with the young, have been admirably blended in the composition of the volume."— *N. Y. Tribune.*

" We have looked through them carefully. They are well written—are moral, sensible, and noble in their ideas—and they contain nothing to offend any parent's creed, for their religiousness is that of every true human heart."— *Boston Post.*

" Here is a beautiful little volume that will make many a young heart sing for joy, when old Santa Claus leaves a copy of it in the stocking in the chimney corner, next Christmas."— *Maine Farmer.*

" A charming collection of poems for children—simple, natural, and graphic; such as the heart of a child dotes upon."— *N. Y. Independent.*

THE PURPOSE OF LIFE

As the shadows were awakening and a scent of the morn was carried on the breeze, I saw an eagle descending from the mountain-tops. It came down without a flutter of the wings into the valley, and there disappeared among the shadows of the black mountains. At the end of the day I saw it return again to its abode among the mountain peaks, far away from the strife, the struggle and the jostle of the world.

So is a man who has seen the vision of Truth, who has, during his strife in the world, established for himself the eternal goal. Though he may wander among the transient things, and lose himself among the shadows, yet all his life will be guided by that goal. As the eagle soars to its abode, so will he soar beyond all sorrows, beyond all fleeting pleasures and passing joys.

The establishment of that eternal goal is of primary importance for one who desires to disentangle himself from all the complications of life — not the goal of another, nor the vision of another, but the goal that is born of his own experience, his own sorrow, suffering, and understanding. Such a goal, when once it is established, will throw light on the confusion of all thought, and thereby make clear the purpose of life.

As a ship that is lost at sea without a compass, so the man without the perception of the goal which is constant and eternal, is lost in this world of confusion. As the captain of a ship establishes the destination of his vessel and by the compass is able to guide his course through stormy nights and dark waters, so the man who has knowl-

edge of his goal can guide his life by that
compass of understanding.

Because the individual does not know his
purpose, he is in a state of uncertainty and
chaos. Because the individual has not solved
his own problem, the problem of the world
has not been solved.

The individual problem is the world
problem. If an individual is unhappy,
discontented, dissatisfied, then the world
around him is in sorrow, discontentment
and ignorance. If the individual has not
found his goal, the world will not find its
goal. You cannot separate the individual
from the world. The world and the
individual are one. If the individual problem
can be solved by understanding, so can
the problem of the world be solved.
Before you can give understanding to
others you have first to understand for
yourself. When you establish the Truth

13

in your heart and mind, there it will abide eternally.

One day in Benares I was going in a boat down the sacred Ganga, watching the people on the river banks worshipping God in search of happiness, in search of their goal and the way of its attainment. I saw one man in deep meditation, forgetting everything around him, holding but the one thought in his mind — to find and to attain the goal. I saw another performing rites required by his system of yoga. I saw another repeating chants, lost to the world and to himself. They were all seeking what you are seeking, what everyone in the world is seeking in moments of deep thought and of great desire. As the boat is carried down the stream by the current, so is everyone carried away by his desires, by his passions and longings, because not one has found or established his purpose. Because the goal has not been established, because the path that leads to that goal has not been found, there is confusion and chaos, there is questioning and doubt in the mind. As long as there is doubt in the mind there is no peace, nor certainty and ecstasy of purpose.

This condition exists throughout the world, but everywhere there is a heart beating and a mind capable of thought. Man everywhere is unconsciously seeking a way to free himself from his narrowness, his pettiness. The end of this search is freedom and eternal happiness. He experiments along many paths, and every path leads to complications. From life to life he wanders, from shrine to shrine, from one creed to another — gathering experience, accepting, rejecting, and again accepting —

thus he goes forward towards that goal which awaits him as it awaits all men. In the process of the accumulation and rejection, he does not know which way to turn for comfort, and when he seeks comfort through any particular channel he is immeshed and entangled. Because there are many interpreters of the Truth, because there are many conflicting paths, beliefs and religions, man is lost in their complexities. As a butterfly that knocks against the window pane, struggling to escape into the fresh air and the open sky, so do men struggle when they have not caught a glimpse of the goal — but it is not hard to establish. It is because they are in darkness that the goal seems far away.

As the potter moulds the clay to the delight of his imagination, so can man

16

mould his life through the desire of his heart. As the earthen vessels are fashioned into beautiful or ugly forms, so life can be made beautiful or ugly according to the purpose which you have established for yourself.

I would help you to that goal which you are seeking, which you desire to attain — the goal which awaits all the peoples of the world, whatever their experiences, thoughts or feelings. Then you will be able to guide yourself through the darkness of the world as a man guides himself of a dark night by the stars.

If you once establish such a goal — which is happiness and hence freedom — life becomes simple. There is no longer confusion, and time and the complications of time disappear. It is because you have not established your goal that the present is as the mountain when the sun has set

— the light fails and the darkness of the
mountain overshadows the valley. Time is
only a binder of life and the moment you
are free you are beyond time.

Then you can guide yourself without
depending upon any authority. Then you
will no longer have fear. Then for you
there will be no conflict of good and evil.
When you have set life free you will find
happiness, which is the only goal, the only
absolute Truth.

HAPPINESS AND DESIRE

Because man has forgotten that the true purpose of his being is to cultivate happiness within himself and in those around him, there is confusion and chaos, and his actions but add to that chaos.

What is it for which everyone in the world is craving and longing? To find happiness. True happiness is neither selfish, nor negative. It is intelligence, the accumulation of all experience; it is Truth, which is eternal. No cloud can hide it nor can any sorrow lessen it. It is such happiness that everyone desires. It is such happiness that I have always desired. I have seen people weighed down with labour, performing great works, accumulating knowledge, struggling to be spiritual, and yet they had forgotten the one thing

— happiness — which alone gives life to the mind and nourishment to the heart. There can be no health except in happiness. He who has not found it will never find Truth, will never bring life to its fulfilment, will never have tranquillity in this world of travail.

If you desire to establish that happiness within yourself, you must make it your goal and then your life will be as the flame which soars heavenwards.

People in search of happiness resort to many things — they will worship at temples and churches, they will gather from books the knowledge of others, they will perform religious rites in the hope of establishing in their minds peace and tranquillity. The desire for happiness is ever gnawing at their hearts.

In the great continent of America they are making the physical predominant in

22

the search for happiness. They say that without physical comfort, without a body that is strong and healthy there cannot be a right development of the emotions. But in trying to establish perfect physical conditions, they are losing sight of other essential things. In India, they go to the opposite extreme and in the search for happiness they neglect altogether the physical.

Look where you will, every human being is seeking happiness. He begins his search in the mere pleasures which come from physical excitement. Then, discovering that this excitement does not satisfy his craving for the lasting happiness, he experiments with other experiences, mental and emotional.

Life is a process of accumulating and discarding, of gathering and setting aside.

23

What you gather you reject, and the more you reject the nearer you are to liberation. By setting aside what you have gained, you acquire the knowledge which will give you strength to shape your purpose, which will give you power ultimately to reach the Kingdom of Happiness which each one of you seeks.

As there is sap in the tree which brings forth foliage for the glory of its being, so in each man there is the spark of divinity which through sorrow, through ecstasy, through struggle, through all the processes of life, grows to perfection, to that state of eternal happiness which is the goal for all, which is the truest spirituality — the greatest gift that anyone can give to another.

You will find this undying, unalterable happiness when you are liberated from the tyrannies of the self, its desires and

24

longings. This is not a goal imposed upon you by another; it is the longing of every human soul, of every individual who is striving, who is in sorrow, who is seeking. It is the spark of this desire which grows into a flame and becomes part of the Eternal Flame, and when you are able to lose yourself in that Flame, you are in the Kingdom of Happiness.

Each must discover his own way of attainment. There is no other truth, no other god, but that goal which each one has established for himself, which cannot be destroyed by the breath of man or by the passing whims of any god.

In what way can you attain this goal and hold this happiness eternally in your heart? If you are a thoughtful person, you will recognize that in everyone there are three different beings — the mind, the emotions

and the body. And if you observe you
will find that each of these beings has a
separate existence of its own and tries to
create and to act independently of the
others, thus causing disharmony. Absolute
happiness comes from the establishment
of harmony between these three. If you
are driving three horses — each desiring
to run independently of the other two —
unless you are able to control them and
drive them all together, you will not reach
your destination.

The mind must have a goal of its own, but
it must be a goal created by you yourself;
otherwise it will lead to superstition.
What is the ultimate goal for the mind?
It is the purification of the self, which
means the development of individual u-
niqueness.
As the seed is forced by the life within

26

it to break through the heavy earth and come into light, so if you are urged by the desire to find freedom, you will break through all limitations which bind you. To gain freedom, great desire is needed. People are afraid of desire, thinking that it is something evil which must be destroyed. But this is a mistaken attitude. Desire is the motive power behind all action. If you would light a great fire to warm and comfort you, you must give fuel to it — feed it with great logs of wood. So if you would fulfil life you must have great desires, for desire brings experience and experience leads to knowledge. If a man knows how to use desire, it will bring him to the freedom for which he longs. If desire is killed or suppressed, there is no possibility of freedom. Most people in the world have intense, burning, vital desires, but instead of utilizing them and training them, they either

27

suppress them or are controlled by them. Without desire there can be no creative work. If you kill desire you become like a piece of dead wood, or else you become an automaton, a machine. Machines have been invented to minimize human labour. Physical problems perhaps may be solved in this way, but mental and emotional problems are more difficult to solve, and because the way to solve these problems is so little understood, religions, creeds, and dogmas have been invented.

If desire gives life it should be encouraged. If desire creates sorrow, through understanding that sorrow must be overcome. Because man does not want to be free, he kills his desires; because he does not want to attain true liberation, he is making of himself a machine. Use desire as a stepping-stone to kindle greater desires, to awaken greater delight and longing.

But intelligence is necessary in order to develop your individual uniqueness, to purify your desires, to realize that self which is the self of all — to realize that absolute union with all things which brings to an end the sense of separation. It is necessary for the mind to be simple, but simplicity does not mean crudeness. We should not turn our back upon the results of progress and evolution, but on the contrary we should utilize them.

A mind that is simple will understand perfection because it is part of perfection itself. A mind that is crooked cannot understand the Truth. A mind that is complicated, that is full of the knowledge of books, though they have their value, is apt to become crystallized. In all great architecture, painting and sculpture, in all the greatest forms of beauty, there is simplicity and there is restraint. Simplicity of the mind is the greatest and most difficult thing to acquire, but in order to be simple you must have had great experience. Simplicity of the truest kind is the highest form of spirituality.

What is the ultimate goal for the emotions? It is affectionate detachment. To be able to love and yet be not attached to anyone or anything is the absolute perfection of emotion.

As a barren tree in winter without leaf or flower to give scent to the morning air, so is a man without love. Those who would attain to Truth, must cultivate, as the gardener cultivates his garden, this flower of affection, which is to give delight, which is to be a source of comfort in disappointment and sorrow. Love — however envious, jealous, tyrannical, selfish it may be at first — is a bud that will grow into

great glory and give the scent of its perfection to every passer-by. Without love
man is as a desert of dry sand, as the
river in the summer time, without water
to nourish its banks. Those who would
attain the perfection of happiness, the
beauty that is hidden from the human eye,
must cultivate this quality of love. You
must love all and yet be detached from
all, for love is necessary to the unfoldment
of life. To cultivate it you must learn to
observe, you must gather experience —
vicariously, or through your own treading
of the sorrowful paths of experience. It
is through experience that you know sympathy, that you are able to give affection to
those who desire it, for if you have never experienced sorrow, then your heart is incapable of sympathy and understanding.
This does not mean that you should taste
of everything. There are many ways of

31

acquiring experience — one is by living in the life of everyone, looking through the eyes of every passer-by and experiencing in imagination his sorrow, his transient pleasures. When you see a drunken man in the street, it should be sufficient to give you the experience of drunkenness; if you see a man in tears, that should give you the experience of grief; if you see a man in joy and in ecstasy, that should give you the experience of joy. We need not all follow one road of knowledge. We give and take from each other. We can gather knowledge from the experience of the whole world and that is sufficient for progress, for culture and refinement. If you would attain to the fulfilment of life, you must have this accumulation of experience, for without experience you cannot arrive at the goal, you cannot unite the beginning and the end. While there

is separation, there is pain, and it is only
in the union with the goal that there is
happiness, that you establish lasting Truth
within yourself. To do that, you must
from the very beginning gather experience
as a man gathers the grain of the field.

If you have no sympathy, no affection,
you can never achieve, you can never
identify yourself with the goal. A mind
that is contented and satisfied will never
acquire sympathy or affection or give
understanding to others. I have watched
people who have greatly desired to help
others but they do not know how to help.
They are incapable of putting themselves
into the place of another and so envisaging
his point of view.

Those who would understand the life
around them, who would see the goal
and thereby establish the Beloved in their
hearts, must develop great love and yet

33

be detached from the bondage of that love. They must have great sympathy and yet not be bound by that sympathy. They must have great desires and yet not be slaves of those desires.

What is the ultimate goal for the body? Beauty. Everyone in the world is seeking for beauty but they seek without understanding. It is essential for the body to be beautiful, but it must not be a mere shell of beauty without beautiful thought and feeling. Restraint is necessary for the body — control without suppression.

These are the essentials for the absolute harmony of the three beings in each of us.

The desire for freedom, the desire to escape from all things, or rather to transcend all things, is necessary for the attainment

34

of perfection. You can only free yourself
if your mind and heart have determined
their purpose in life and are continually
struggling towards it, never yielding to
those things which create barriers between
yourself and your goal.

To attain perfection, to walk towards the
goal of Truth which is eternal happiness
for all, at whatever stage of evolution you
may be, it is necessary to be rid of the
binding narrow traditions that are born
out of blind belief and have no touch
with life.

As when the rains come, only those who
have prepared their fields and removed
the weeds will have the full produce of
their labour, the full benefit of the rain,
so, if you would have the Beloved always
with you, you must remove from your
mind and heart the complicated ideas,
traditions, and narrow points of view

which are as weeds that kill true understanding. For without understanding there
can be no coöperation with life.

U N D E R S T A N D I N G

For the well-being of the mind and heart, understanding is as essential as a warm fire on a cold night.

People imagine that they can attain by some miraculous process, that they can find Truth by the mere outward form of worship, that they can discover their goal by the continual repetition of prayers and chants, or by the performance of *yoga*, *puja* and other rites. You can only discover that which you desire, that for which your heart longs, and for which your mind craves, by yourself, through the purification of the heart and mind.

If you would understand Truth you must remove from your heart those stones and weeds which strangle its full growth.

Where there is narrowness of mind and limitation of heart, Truth cannot enter.

39

If you would climb to that height where there are eternal snows, you must leave behind you the accumulation of your possessions, you must be hardened and well trained, and your heart must be filled with the desire of attainment.

For those who have no fixed purpose there is renunciation and self-sacrifice, there is sorrow, grief and pain, endless struggle and violent dissatisfaction. But for those who have the fixed purpose to attain the Truth which is the unfoldment of life — though they may dwell in the valley of the shadows — there is no sacrifice, there is no struggle.

Because you have no fixed purpose, all the shadows of the valley entice you, wrap you in their soft fogs, so that you lose the ecstasy of life. But if you have established your goal, which is the goal of the world — the attainment of the Kingdom of

Happiness through freedom from all experience — then you can control the future, then you are the creator of that which you desire. If you can pass through the valley of the shadows with eyes eternally fixed upon the mountain-top, then you can have all experience without creating barriers between yourself and the goal. This is the understanding of life which will bring order out of chaos and it is for that purpose that the Beloved has come. As the true artist, who by his imagination creates beauty out of the chaos around him, out of the confusion which exists in the world, so the Beloved, Truth, creates order in the mind and heart of those who understand. When you understand, you will have solved the problem of your daily life. If there is no struggle within to free yourself from the cage of sorrow and pain, from the limitations which cause confusion, then,

however much I may knock at the door
of your heart, there will be no response.
But the moment you yourself are dissatisfied, the moment you yourself desire to
escape and to attain liberation, then you
yourself seek the source of Truth.
Those who seek for an understanding of
life must fix their inward perception on
eternal Truth, which is the unfolding of life.

To those who live in and have their being
in the valley, the mountains are mysterious, hard, cruel, eternally aloof. The
mountains never change; they are ever
constant, never yielding. So it is with Truth.
To those who live in the valley of shadows,
of transient things, Truth seems terrible,
hard and cruel.
Everywhere, among all people, there is a
search · for something hidden, for some
realization which will give wisdom, greater

knowledge, greater vision, greater understanding: this the people call Truth.

They think that Truth lies hidden in some
distant place, away from life, away from
joy, away from sorrow. But Truth is life,
and with an understanding of life there
is born an understanding of Truth. When
you are fulfilling life with understanding,
you are the master of Truth.

Though there is at the present time a
revolt against tradition and the established
order of things, against morality in the
narrow sense; yet the majority of people
still judge and try to understand life from
the prejudiced point of view of a limited
and settled mind. A Hindu will only recognize Truth when it is presented to him
through the medium of Hinduism, and so
it is with the Christian and the Buddhist.
But Truth is never contained in a particular form or medium. Truth can only

be understood with an unbiassed mind, capable of detachment and pure judgment. As every human being is divine, so every individual in the world should be his own master, his own absolute ruler and guide. But if he would guide himself intelligently, he must be able to judge all things with an open mind and not reject what he does not understand because he is prejudiced.

Truth is the power within each one of you which urges you on to attainment. It is the consummation of all intelligence. It is Absolute. There is no God except the man who has purified himself and so has attained to Truth.

When you bind life to beliefs and traditions, to codes of morality, you kill life. In order to keep alive, vital, ever-changing, ever-growing, as the tree that is ever putting out new leaves, you must give to life the opportunities, the nourishment which will strengthen it and make it grow. When life desires to find its freedom, the only way by which it can attain is through experience.

There can be no understanding of life, which is Truth, when there is not the thrill, the agony, the suffering, the continual upheaval, discouragement and encouragement of life.

In the olden days, especially in India, those who desired to find Truth imagined that they could discover the way by withdrawing from the aching world, from the transient things, from the shadow of the real, by the destruction of the physical. But now you have to face life as it is, for you can only conquer life when you have a complete and not a partial understanding of it.

Once there was a man who kept all the

45

windows of his house well closed except one, hoping that through that window alone the sunlight would come, but it never came. That is what those people are doing who are bound by tradition, by narrow sectarian beliefs, and who think that Truth is contained in any of those beliefs. You cannot bind life, which is the Truth, by anything, for life must be free and untrammelled. If you do not understand that the purpose of life is freedom, then you are only gilding the bars of your cage by the invention of theories, of creeds, of philosophies and religions.

The basis of all these innumerable beliefs is fear. You are afraid for your salvation, you are afraid to test your own knowledge, and hence you rely on the assertions, on the authority of another.

In order to be happy need we have religions? In order to love need we build

temples? In order to fulfil the self need
we worship a personal god?
You must give to the suffering world —
not beliefs, creeds, dogmas — but new
understanding which comes from intelligent
coöperation with Nature, through observation of all the events of daily life.

Those who would understand Truth, who
would give of their heart and their mind
to that Truth, must first have grown in
experience. Then experience will guide
them, for experience gives intelligence, and
intelligence is the accumulation of all experience. The web of life is spun out of
common things and the common things
are experience.
Learn from every event, from every activity in daily life, and assimilate the experience every moment of the day.
You go to Temples or to Churches or

to other places of worship, and there you imagine that you are purified. But does that purification stand the test of daily life? Your theories, your superficial knowledge of life do not help you at moments of crisis. When death comes and takes away your friend, your beliefs and theories do not help you to overcome your loneliness and the sense of separation. You will only overcome it if the poison of separation has been destroyed, and you can only destroy that sense of separation by observing others in sorrow, in pain, and in pleasure like yourself, and finding that in suffering as well as in pleasure there is unity.

No one can develop that power which dwells within you but you yourself, for that power grows by experience. But experience alone, undirected by the goal you would attain, produces chaos, the chaos which prevails in the world at present.

48

UNDERSTANDING

Without the understanding of the purpose of life there is bound to be chaos.

The first demand upon those who would seek the understanding of true happiness is that they should have the burning longing to be free from all things, to gain that freedom which comes when you are beyond the need for further experience because you have passed through all experience.

If you would understand what I mean by the freedom of life, you must establish for yourself the goal which is liberation even from life itself.

For the understanding of life you must have revolt, dissatisfaction and great discontentment. Many people in the world imagine that they have found Truth by adopting some theory or other, and hence that they have solved the whole problem of life. Contentment without understanding is like a pool covered with green scum, which does not reflect the bare eye of heaven. It is very easy to be ignorantly discontented, but to be discontented and to revolt intelligently is a divine gift. Revolt with intelligence, with understanding, is as a great river that is full of power.

Revolt is essential in order to escape from the narrowness of tradition, from the binding influences of belief, of theories. If you would understand the Truth, you must be in revolt so that you may escape from all these — from the books, from the theories, from the gods, from superstitions, from everything which is not of your own.

If you would understand the meaning of my words, then throw aside all your mental conceptions of life and begin again from the very beginning. Then you will see for yourself how life works, how life, which is the accumulation of all experience, speaks through that voice which we call intuition, which guides you and helps you on the onward path.

I would urge you to be free — free from the very gods whom you worship, from the very beings whom you hold dear, because freedom is necessary for the growth of the soul, and without freedom there is decay.

Because you do not wish to be free, you seek comfort, and comfort is like the shadow of a tree; it varies according to the sun from moment to moment, and those who seek comfort must move from one abode to another. Comfort cannot dwell with understanding.

The man who seeks comfort, who searches for the satisfaction of the moment, will never find real and lasting joy, for the momentary comfort is as transitory as the flower that is born of a morning and withers at the ending of the day.

When a pond is not touched with the breath of air, the waters become stagnant, and no animal comes to it to slake its thirst. But when the fresh winds come and breathe on its face, then animals and human beings alike can quench their thirst. So if there is not in you the fresh wind of desire for freedom from all things, you will not find the Truth which alone can remove the thirst of the world.

When you are free, as the bird in the skies, your life becomes simple. Life is complicated only when there is limitation. Then you need traditions and beliefs to uphold you. But when you desire to be free from all things, then you break away from the old order and enter upon that new life which will lead you towards perfection which is liberation and happiness.

When you are able to become a flame of revolt, then the means to reach that Kingdom will be found.

We have to create a miracle of order in this century of chaos and superstition. But first we have to create order in ourselves, a lasting order which is not based on fear or on authority.

I have found and established for myself that which is eternal, and it is my work to create order in your mind, so that you will no longer depend on outward authority, no longer be the slave of superstition or of those trivialities which hold life in bondage, and divide you from your goal.

Because you have no true purpose in life there is chaos within you; there is misery without understanding, strife without purpose, struggle in ignorance. But when you have established the goal of the Beloved in your heart and mind, there is understanding in your life. There may still be struggle but it will be with understanding and there will be greater love and greater happiness. Establish therefore within you that which is eternal, and the present shadows will pass away.

When you have established the Beloved in your heart, the source and the end are united and time no longer exists, for you hold eternity within you.

When you have established the Beloved in your heart, you are ready to face the open seas, where there are great storms, and the strong breezes which quicken life.

Because you have the Beloved in your heart, you must be as a lighthouse on a dark shore, to guide those who are still enshrouded in their own darkness.

Of what value is your understanding, of what value are your high and noble thoughts, your pure life, if you do not help those who are in constant pain, who are in darkness, and in confusion? Of what value is the Truth you have seen if you are not able to give of that Truth to those who are hungering and thirsting after the eternal?

Because you have understood, be courageous with that understanding, and give of your life to those who are in darkness.

THE SEARCH

If you would see life as a clear picture,
you must, by discriminating and select-
ing from your many experiences,
gather the knowledge which will help you
to the attainment of your goal. Life cannot
be separated from thought, feeling and
action, and when you understand life as
a whole, using all experience as a ladder
on which to climb, you attain.

My purpose is to make clear to you your
own desires, to strengthen your own unique
growth towards perfection. But if you
merely obey me or use me as an authority,
as a stepping-stone towards your goal, you
will fail, because it will not be your own
desire that urges you. Whereas, if you
strengthen the understanding of your own
desire and use all experience to that end,
no one can destroy or take away that
which you have gained.

As from out of a fire there comes forth a spark which can in its turn light a great flame, springing heavenwards, so in every man there is born the spark of desire, and I would strengthen that desire in you that you may be able for yourself to light the fire which is necessary for the fulfilment of life.

To follow another, whosoever he may be, is to me the very negation of what I hold to be true. Worship is contrary to all my ideas — especially worship of individuals — and if you regard me as an authority when this form of mine passes away, you will again be bound to the same wheel of limitation. I do not want followers, I do not want disciples, I do not want praise or worship of any kind. I need nothing from anyone.

The time when one left the world and went away to a secluded spot, to a monastery, is past. The time for open life and clear understanding has come and I would speak of that understanding which I have found. I would show you how I have found my Beloved, how the Beloved is established in me, how the Beloved is the Beloved of all, and how the Beloved and I are one so that there can be no separation either now or at any time.

I have long been in revolt from all things, from the authority of others, from the instruction of others, from the knowledge of others; I would not accept anything as Truth until I found the Truth myself. I never opposed the ideas of others but I would not accept their authority, their theory of life. Until I was in that state of revolt, until I became dissatisfied with everything, with every creed, with every dogma and belief, I was not able to find the Truth. Until I was able to destroy these things by constant struggle to understand what lies behind them, I was not able to attain the Truth I sought.

Naturally I did not think of all these things while I was young — they grew in me unconsciously. But now I can place all the events of my life in their proper order and see in what manner I have developed to attain my goal, and have become my goal.

For long I have searched for that goal, and during my search I have watched people trapped in their desires, as a fly is caught in the web of a spider. Ever since I was able to think I have watched people absorbed in their own thoughts, suffocated by the futility of life. Wherever I went I saw people who believed that their happiness consisted in the multitude of possessions. I saw people who had all the comforts of this world, and yet their lives were in confusion, because they were enslaved by these things. I saw people who loved greatly and yet were bound by their love, for they had not found the way to give love and yet be free. I saw people who were wise in knowledge; and yet they were bound by their very learning. I saw people who were steeped in religion and yet they were bound by their traditions and by their fear of the unknown.

I saw the wise withdraw from the world into their own seclusion, and the ignorant caught up in their own labours.

Watching people thus, I have seen that they build for themselves walls of prejudice, walls of belief, walls of credulous thought, walls of great fear against which they fight, trying to escape from the very walls they themselves have built. Watching all people, I have seen how useless is their struggle if they are not free from the very gods they worship, from the interpreters who would guide them. Each guide, each interpreter of the Truth translates that Truth according to his own limited vision. If you depend on the interpreter for your understanding, you will only learn the Truth according to his limitations. But if you establish the goal for yourself, if you strengthen your own desire for Truth and test the keenness of that desire by observation, by welcoming sorrow and experience, then you need have no mediators, then there need exist nothing between you and your goal, between you and the Truth.

I would that I could make you certain of the Truth, for Truth is greater than every book of every religion, greater than every belief that you hold dear. But because you do not understand, Truth appears to you as something fearsome, an enemy

64

to be conquered, and because of this fear you seek a mediator. But if you have a pure heart and a mind that is full with understanding, you do not need *gurus*, mediators who must inevitably condition, limit the Truth.

Ever since I was young I have observed these things, and I have never allowed myself to be caught up in any of these confusions. Because I have established my goal, because I have always regarded myself as a boat on the stream, having no connection with the land where there is confusion, I have attained, and now I would share my experience with others. I would help those who are confused to make their minds and hearts simple in their desire for attainment.

Ever since I was a boy I have been, as most young people are, or should be, in revolt. Nothing satisfied me. I listened,

I observed, I wanted something beyond mere phrases, the *maya* of words. I wanted to discover and to establish for myself my goal. I did not want to rely on anyone. I do not remember the time when I was being moulded in my boyhood, but I can look back and see how nothing satisfied me.

When I went to Europe for the first time I lived among people who were wealthy and well educated, who held positions of social authority; but whatever their dignities or distinctions, they could not satisfy me. I was in revolt also against theosophists with all their jargon, their theories, their meetings, and their explanations of life. When I went to a meeting, the lecturers repeated the same ideas which did not satisfy me or make me happy. I went to fewer and fewer meetings, I saw less and less of the people who merely

66

repeated the ideas of Theosophy. I ques-
tioned everything because I wanted to
find out for myself.

I walked about the streets, watching the
faces of people who perhaps watched me
with even greater interest. I went to
theatres; I saw how people amused themselves, trying to forget their unhappiness,
thinking that they were solving their problems by drugging their hearts and minds
with superficial excitement.

I saw people with political, social or
religious power — and yet they did not
have that one essential thing in their lives,
which is happiness.

I attended labour meetings, communist
meetings, and listened to what their leaders
had to say. They were generally protesting
against something. I was interested, but
they did not give me satisfaction.

By observation of one type and another

67

I gathered experience vicariously. Within everyone there was a latent volcano of unhappiness and discontentment. I passed from one pleasure to another, from one amusement to another, in search of happiness and found it not. I watched the amusements of the young people, their dances, their dresses, their extravagances, and I saw that they were not happy with the happiness which I was seeking. I watched people who had very little in life, who wanted to tear down those things which others had built up. They thought that they were solving life by destroying and building differently and yet they were unhappy.

I saw people who desired to serve going into those quarters where the poor and the degraded live. They desired to help but were themselves helpless. How can you cure another of disease if you are yourself a victim of that disease?

68

I saw people satisfied with the stagnation
which is unproductive, uncreative — the
bourgeois type which never struggles to
be above the surface or falls below it and
so feels its weight.
I read books on philosophy, on religion,
biographies of great people, and yet they
could not give me what I wanted. I wanted
to be so certain, so positive, in my attitude
towards life that nothing could disturb me.

Then I came to India and I saw that the
people there were deluding themselves
equally, carrying on the same old traditions, treating women cruelly. At the same
time they called themselves very religious
and painted their faces with ashes. In India
they may have the most sacred books in
the world, they may have the greatest
philosophies, they may have constructed
wonderful temples in the past, but none

of these was able to give me what I wanted. Neither in Europe nor in India could I find happiness.

Still I wandered always in search of this happiness which I knew must exist. This was not a merely intellectual or emotional conviction. It was like the hidden perfection which cannot be described, but of the existence of which you are certain. You cannot ask a bud how it opens, in what manner it gives forth its scent, at what time of the morning it unfolds itself to the sun. But if you watch carefully, if you observe keenly, you will discover for yourself the hidden beauty of perfection.

Still lacking the fixed purpose from which comes the delight of living, I went to California. Circumstances forced me there because my brother was ill. There among the hills we lived in a small house in

complete retirement, doing everything for
ourselves. If you would discover Truth
you must for a time withdraw from the
world. In that retired spot my brother
and I talked much together. We meditated,
trying to understand, for meditation of
the heart is understanding.

There I was naturally driven within myself
and I learned that as long as I had no
definite goal or purpose in life, I was,
like the rest of mankind, tossed about as
a ship on a stormy sea. With that in my
mind, after rejecting all lesser things, I
established for myself my goal. I wanted
to enter into eternal happiness, I wanted
to become the very goal. I wanted to
drink from the source of life. I wanted
to unite the beginning and the end. I fixed
that goal as my Beloved and that Beloved
is Life, the Life of all things. I wanted to
destroy the separation that exists between

man and his goal. I said to myself that as long as there is this void of separation between myself and my goal there is bound to be misery, disturbance and doubt. There will be authority which I must obey, to which I must yield. As long as there is separation between you and me there is unhappiness for us both. So I set about destroying all the barriers that I had previously erected. I began to reject, to renounce, to set aside what I had gathered, and little by little I approached my goal.

When my brother died, the experience it brought me was great — not the sorrow — sorrow is momentary and passes away, but the joy of experience remains. If you understand life rightly then death becomes an experience out of which you can build your house of perfection, your house of delight. When my brother died, that gap of separation still existed in me; I saw him once or twice after death but that did not satisfy me. How can you be satisfied alone? You may invent phrases, you may have great knowledge of books; but as long as there is within you separation and loneliness, there is sorrow. Because I desired to establish life within myself, because I desired to become united with the goal, I struggled. Life is a process of struggle, of continuous gathering of the dust of experience.

If you are lost on a dark night and you see a distant light, you make your way towards that light with bleeding feet, through bogs, through pitfalls, through difficulties, because you know that the light indicates a human dwelling. So have I walked and struggled towards that light which is my goal, which is the goal of all humanity, because it is humanity itself.

All the pitfalls, all the things which entangle, all the things which hurt, are transient and pass away. I suffered but I set about to free myself from everything that bound me, till in the end I became united with the Beloved, I entered into the sea of liberation, and established that liberation within me.

The simple union with the Beloved, the direct way of attainment, which is the eternal way, gives ecstasy to life. If you search for Truth in the realms of *maya*, in the realm of the intellect or of mere emotionalism, or in the physical sense-world alone, you will never find it. Yet when you have found it you realize that it is contained in them all. You cannot separate life from any expression of life and yet you must be able to distinguish between life and its expressions. Because at first I tried to separate life from the

74

goal, because to me life was one thing and knowledge another, everything became confused and I turned for support to tradition, to comfort, to self-contentment and satisfaction. When you perceive the light of your goal, you are guided by it as a ship is guided by a lighthouse on a dark shore. When you have seen that vision of perfection, that hidden beauty which cannot be explained in words, which is beyond intellectual theories and mere emotional excitement, it will act as your eternal guide, it will shed its light upon your path and whatever your experience or lack of experience may be, you will attain. Attainment is not for the few but for all, at whatever stage of evolution they may be. You can perceive the Beloved when you have learnt to translate the ordinary sorrows and pleasures of life into terms of eternal Truth. If you can interpret all experience in the light of your goal, then you will become united with that goal.

Because I am united eternally, inseparably, with my Beloved — who is the Beloved of all, who is yourself — I would show you the way, because you are in pain, in sorrow, in doubt. But I can only be a signpost for you. You must have the strength of your own desire to attain. You must experience the pain and the sorrow in your own self. You must strive for yourself. Your desire must come from your very soul. It must be the result of your own experience, for by that alone will you attain.

By telling you of my attainment I do not wish to create authority because if I create authority in your mind I shall destroy your own perception of the Truth. I want to make you breathe the fresh

air of the mountains, but if you seek my
authority you will remain in your dark
valley of limitation. It is much easier for
you to follow and worship blindly than
to understand and so become truly free.
Until I was able to identify myself with
the goal, which is the Beloved of all,
which is the Source and the End of all,
I did not want to say that I had found
and, in finding, had become the Beloved.
Till I was able to unite with the eternal
I could not pass on the Truth to others;
till I was certain of having found the
lasting goal I did not want to say that I
was the Teacher. Now that I have found,
now that I have established the Beloved
within myself, now that the Beloved is
myself, I would give you of the Truth
— not that it should be received with
authority, but with understanding. It does
not matter whether you accept or reject

it. When a flower opens and gives its scent, it does not heed if the passer-by does not delight in its fragrance.

I have painted my picture on the canvas and I want you to examine it critically, not blindly. I want you to create because of that picture a new picture for yourself. I want you to fall in love with the picture, not with the painter, to fall in love with the Truth and not with him who brings the Truth. Fall in love with yourself and then you will fall in love with everyone.

In order to attain liberation it is not necessary to join any organization, any religion, because they are binding, they are limiting, they hold you to a particular form of worship and belief. If you long for freedom you will fight, as I have fought, against authority of any kind, for authority is the antithesis of spirituality.

78

If I were to use authority today and you accepted my authority, it would not make you free, you would be merely following the freedom of another. In following the freedom of another, you are binding yourself more strongly to the wheel of limitation. Do not allow your mind or your heart to be bound by anything or by anyone. If you do, you will establish another religion, another temple. While destroying one set of beliefs you will establish another set of beliefs. I am fighting against all traditions that bind, all worship that narrows, all following that corrupts the heart. If you would find that freedom to which I would point the way, you will begin, as I began, by being discontented, by being in revolt, in inner dissent with everything about you. You frequently use the phrase "We will obey our leaders". Who are your leaders? I never want to be a leader. I never want to have authority. I want you to become your own leaders.

Life is simple and magnificent, lovely and divine, but you want all the beauty and the freshness of the dawn and of the still night to be caught and held in a narrow circle so that you can worship it. Go down to the sea-beach of an evening when the fresh breezes are blowing and all the blades of grass are in motion and the particles of sand are flying about and the trees are waving their branches, and the waves of the sea are breaking over each other. You want to gather and bind all that beauty into a narrow temple. You need have no beliefs in order to live nobly. And yet you say, "I must worship gods, I must perform rites, I must go to shrines, I must follow this and do that". It is an eternal *must*. That way of living is not living at all.

Whatever you do, do not create another temple around me: I shall not be held within it. I want to be your companion with the freshness of the breeze. I want to free you from your own limitations, to encourage within you individual creation, individual perfection, individual uniqueness. The self can only be purified and truly transcended when it has developed its own individual uniqueness to perfection; not when it is held in limitations, bound by traditions, by forms, and by all the unnecessary paraphernalia which you think essential to your well-being.

I remember a story written by a Norwegian — the hero of that story in search for freedom and happiness joins one religion after another and worships one God after another, performs one ceremony after another, and still he cannot find what he

seeks. At length he becomes a Buddhist
and drops his physical body and enters
Nirvana. He enters the Nirvana of the
books and there he sees all the gods of
all the religions seated and conversing with
each other. They offer him a vacant seat.
This hero appears as a flame, but this
flame does not want to be caught, and
while all the gods try to catch hold of him
he disappears. The gods cannot follow him
because even gods themselves are bound.
Do not be bound by me or by anyone.
Happiness is within yourself.

I set out to find for myself the purpose
of life and I found it without the authority
of another. I have entered that sea of
liberation and happiness in which there
is no limitation or negation because it is
the fulfilment of life.
Because after my long journey towards

attainment and perfection I have attained that perfection and established it in my heart, and because my mind is tranquil and eternally liberated as the flame, I would give of that understanding to all.

STAND IN YOUR OWN STRENGTH

Everyone in the world is concerned with the search for that Truth which will satisfy them eternally, but in that search each one contends against another; and hence there is confusion, struggle and pain. They lack the certainty of purpose which will determine their course through life and so rely on another for their comfort, well-being and understanding.

Because they admit that they are weak, because they maintain that they cannot stand without the support of another, they have been given crutches that will support them momentarily, instead of developing their own strength to go forward in search of the pure waters of Truth.

If you would find that Truth, you must put aside all those things upon which you

87

have leaned for support and look within
for that everlasting spring. It cannot be
brought to you through any outward
channel.

In search of the Truth that shall sustain,
uphold, and guide you, you have looked
outwards and sought for it objectively,
and thus have been lost in the shadows
of manifestation. To find that spring of
Truth you must look within, you must
purify your heart and mind.

You say to me, "You are different; you have
attained, and because you have attained,
these comforts are unnecessary for *you*".
No, friend, because you desire to attain,
these things are unnecessary for *you*.
Because I have leaned on crutches to
support me, I know the uselessness of
crutches. When you have passed along a
dangerous narrow path, and you have often
slipped, and had to climb again — surely

88

you would say to your fellow travellers, "Beware of these things, do not walk on the edge, walk rather in the middle, keeping your balance, and do not be led away so that you fall over the precipice".

Because I know that your comforts only weaken you, I tell you to throw them away. Because I have been entangled in complexities, because I have been held in bondage, I urge you to escape into freedom. Because I have found a simple and direct path, I would tell you of it. If I had relied for my happiness on others, if I had been caught up in grandiloquent phrases, in the worship of images or persons, or in the shadows of temples, I should not have found that Truth which I sought. Not in the worship of externals do you find the spring of Truth, but in the adoration of Truth itself.

Because you imagine that without all these

complications of beliefs and systematized thoughts which are called religions, you cannot find Truth, that very thought is preventing you from finding it. If you would climb to a great height, if you would go far, you do not carry on your shoulders great burdens. In like manner, if you would attain liberation, you do not cling to the burdens which you have accumulated throughout the ages. You must put aside those things which you have gained and reach out for further understanding.

In search of the waters that shall quench your thirst, if you are wise you will not act in haste. Through haste you find nothing. By patient understanding, by careful watching that you may not be caught up in things that are trivial, unessential, you find that which you seek. It is difficult for you to realize that your own understanding

dwells within, that your happiness lies
within yourself, because you have been
accustomed to look to objective things
for your understanding and your Truth.
Invite doubt; for doubt is as a precious
ointment: though it burns, it shall heal
greatly; and by inviting doubt, by putting
aside those things which you have understood, by transcending your acquirements,
your understandings, you will find the
Truth.

THE HIDDEN WELL

When the fountain is sealed and the spring is shut up, to open that fountain and release that spring you must dig deep, and thereby disturb the earth. In like manner and for the same purpose there must be disturbance within you if you would find Truth. As the waters are hidden in the dry lands, so is Truth hidden in your heart. I would dig in each of you a well that shall nourish and sustain you, but to dig deep, you must uproot greatly, to have great depth of water you must delve deeply into the earth. The process of digging creates discontentment and revolt, and the destruction of useless things. Love Truth for its own beauty, do right because you yourself desire to do it, and develop the inward perception of true understanding. If you follow without understanding, you will betray the Truth; and because I hold that Truth with such care, with such gratitude for its loveliness, I want you not to betray it. For this reason I am creating revolt within you, I am digging deep to discover the waters that shall nourish you, the Truth that shall give you tranquillity, the Truth that shall give you ecstasy of purpose in this world of confusion. If you merely repeat after me new phrases instead of the old, that repetition will not show the way to Truth. There must be a vital change in the mind and in the heart before that inward perception of Truth which is the true understanding of life, can be developed. Do not settle down more comfortably in your already comfortable attitude of mind, for satisfaction and contentment do not lead to Truth, neither do they bring happiness.

Become a genius by developing your own individual uniqueness. The genius of one man can never be complete, the genius which is the outcome of the individual uniqueness of many, which all have helped to produce, will alone be perfect. If you would create greatly, if you would have the creation last eternally, you must develop your own individual uniqueness, your own perfection, with the understanding of the Truth, and not imitate the perfection of another.

BE IN LOVE WITH LIFE

During the time of winter, every tree looks forward to the warm airs of the spring, but when that spring comes, if there is no life in the tree it will not put forth green foliage, flowers and fruit. I am telling you of that life which is in all things, and in keeping that life pure, strong and vital, you will find happiness, and not in limiting that life and placing it in bondage. Everyone in the world is more concerned with the branches and leaves of the tree than with the sap which gives vitality to the whole tree. I am concerned with the life of the tree, and not with the branch, the leaf, the flower and the fruit, because I hold that as long as the life in the tree is healthy, its expression is bound to be beautiful. In the same way if the life in you is strong,

101

vital and pure, you will attain to that Truth which is unlimited and cannot be conditioned. If you seek to condition it, it is betrayed.

You are all concerned with the appearance of the tree, with the pruning of its branches, with the examination of its leaves; you are intoxicated with its perfume and you are not pleased when you are called back to the consideration of that which produces your tree with its perfume, its leaves and its branches. As there is no life in a dead branch, it is broken by the winter winds and drops away. Such will be the man who does not put life before all lesser things, who does not release life from its bondage, from the trivialities that have been imposed upon it. In order to free life you must be in love with life. You would much rather adore an image than worship life itself.

Do not put aside what I am saying with

a shrug of your shoulders, but listen dil-
igently and you will understand greatly.
If you are prejudiced, if you are determined
to twist life to suit your particular beliefs,
your particular branch of the expression
of life, then you will not find the Truth.
In order to release that spring which will
develop into a torrent and hence carry you
to the attainment of liberation which is
Truth, which is the fulfilment of life, you
must discover what is essential for your
understanding, and set aside all those things
which are of secondary importance.
You will be unhappy; you will struggle;
you will have to go through disappoint-
ments, anxieties, great agonies, if you place
the unessential before the essential. That
is what you are all doing because to you
life and the freedom of life is not important.
When you are in love with life you will
invite sorrow, doubt, every experience, in

order that you may conquer every experience, that you may break the bondages which you have placed on life.

To find the Truth, you must give up the worship of the image and fall in love with life. Then you will become immortal. The fear of death disappears in him who is in love with life and who sees that life in the eyes of his neighbour. Be in love with life and loyal to life and not to persons, because the worship of personalities does not lead you to Truth. Truth does not belong to any individual, Truth does not belong to any religion, Truth cannot be found in the dark sanctuary of temples, nor in the well-lit halls of organized societies; neither can it be found in books nor in ceremonies. I would bring you to the understanding of Truth, but you would much rather have me repeat what you have heard a hundred times. You would much rather that I put you to sleep, lull you in comfort, than awaken in you the desire to shatter all things, to discover life.

If you would discover the cause for all the beauty of the world, for all the dancing shadows, do not be caught up in the illusion of the expressions of life, but rather seek for that Truth which is life itself by being in love with life.

T I M E

For those who have discovered Truth and attained the fulfilment of life — which is happiness and liberation — time and the complications of time have ceased. But those who are still bound to the yoke of experience are limited by the past, present and future.

You who would discover the Truth which is absolute and infinite must realize that you are the product of the past and the outcome of your own creation. You are bringing forth out of your self that which you have sown in the past. And as man is the product of the past, so by his actions of today he can control the future. Tomorrow depends upon today, and therefore today determines tomorrow. By controlling the future you become the master of the future. You bring the future to the

109

present. Everyone throughout the world
is bound by the traditions, the fears, the
shame, the beliefs, the morality of the
past. If you are constantly looking back-
wards, you will never discover Truth.
The discovery of eternal Truth lies always
ahead of you. If you truly understand
this, you will not cling to the past. You
will not be always conditioned by the
thoughts, the actions, the feelings, the
ethics of the past, because therein is
stagnation and the bondage of life. Cut
away the bondage of the past as a woodman
cuts his way through a dark forest to find
the open spaces and fresh breezes. For
the past always binds, however glorious,
however well seasoned, however fruitful
it may have been, and the man who would
be free must look eternally forward.

If you would walk, and build, and create
in the shelter of eternity, you must not

bring the past into conflict with the present, but must invite the future and thereby bring that future into conflict with the present.

Because your mind and heart are bound by traditions and beliefs, by the sacred books of the past, by the dark shadows of temples, and remembered gods, you do not understand either the present or the future. Time, as man understands it, is dividing you from your goal. Therefore, to bring time to naught, you must so live now that you are the master of the future, so that the future becomes the present. People love to think of themselves as being glorified in the future, or resting on the laurels of what they have been in the past. What a comforting idea! The belief in your greatness in some distant future will not help you to deal with life in the present, when you are struggling, when there is confusion in your mind and heart.

Not in the distant future did I want to be great, but I desired to be happy in the present, I wanted to be free in the present, I wanted to be beyond all the limitations of time. So I invited the future into the present, and hence I have conquered the future.

Do not live in the future nor in the dead things of yesterday, but live rather in the immediate now, with the understanding that you are a product of the past, and that by your actions of today you can control tomorrow and so become the master of time, the master of evolution, and hence the master of perfection.

Then you will live with greater intensity, then every second will count and every moment will be of value. But you are frightened of such a present. You would much rather be conditioned by the past because you have a dread of the future.

But the future is not fearsome to those who walk in the way of understanding. If you would attain to the fulfilment of life you must invite the future to the present and thereby create a conflict within yourself. Through contentment you do not find happiness, but a state of stagnation. If you would know true happiness there must first be that inward conflict, which will bring forth in you the flower of life.

Put aside the past with all its glories, beautiful and terrible, all its traditions, wide and yet so conditioned, all its moralities that strangle life, and look into your own heart and mind to discover what lies before you in the future. For as you are the product of the past, and as you can control the future, so the future becomes the present and you live in that present.

FORMLESS CREATION

From these Camps you will go away to all parts of the world carrying with you that which you have understood, and carrying with you, alas, also that which you have not understood. If that which you have not understood be the stronger, because of its strength it will pervert that which you have understood. I would give you the flower of understanding which shall know no decay, so that you may keep it ever with you.

Truth is like a flame without definite form, it varies from moment to moment. No man can describe it, but by the light of Truth alone you must walk, if you would keep that flower of understanding with you always.

Because you will go away with phrases, with words, with half ideas, the full beauty of manifestation will escape you. I have heard people say, "I must give up music. I must no longer admire painting. I must no longer enjoy the shade of a tree and the glory of sunset, nor the reflection of the swallow of a still evening on the face of the waters." If that is what you understand when I say that life is more important than its expressions, you will destroy the beauty of the expression, and then you will have to create that beauty again. Do you think that there is so much beauty around us in expression, in manifestation, only to be destroyed, to be put aside and not be admired?

As the water is necessary for the beauty of the lotus, and as the lotus makes the waters beautiful, so, when the expression of life is destroyed, when it is made hideous and horrible to behold, then life itself, which is in each one, becomes perverted, mutilated and ugly. So, friend, do not cease to admire beauty. Do not hold back the laughter that awakens in your heart when you see a dancing leaf. Do not thwart the expressions of life by misunderstanding the purpose of life. To bring that expression to perfection, to its fulfilment, life must be free, life must not be bound by traditions, by your stagnating moralities and beliefs. The expressions of life will then be naturally beautiful.

There have been many thousand people at these Camps and what could they not do in the world if they all understood! They could change the face of the world tomorrow. Its expression would become different because new life had been brought to it.

That is what I long to do. That is the only desire that burns in my heart. Because I see sadness and corruption, pain and

119

suffering, passing ecstasies and passing fantasies, I would awaken life and bring it to its perfect fulfilment. You who are going away must realize your responsibility. Truth is not to be played with, nor to be corrupted by misunderstanding, but to be developed with full understanding of the purpose of life. If you have caught a glimpse of Truth, if you are walking on the path of understanding, you can change the thought and feeling of the world; but before you can change the world, you must change your own heart and mind. For this reason you have gathered together; for this reason you have been shaken to the very foundation — as I hope — of your structure. You have come to discover, in the light of the Truth, that which is lasting, that which shall stand against the storm, and distinguish it from that which is unimportant, trivial and to be set aside.

For that reason I have urged you to invite doubt, and to examine with understanding all that you have gathered through the ages. Adversity is as a furnace through which everyone must pass. Great struggles, great sorrows and great ecstasies unfold the Truth in its sublimity, in its simplicity. To welcome adversity — not thrust upon you by another — you must invite doubt. If doubt unconsciously insinuates itself into your heart, it will not purify it. You can only purify it by deliberately inviting doubt.

Those who would attain greatly, who would understand truly, must invite the future, and let that future come into conflict with the fruit of the past, which is the present. But you do not want to do that. All your questions, all your thoughts and feelings have been about the past. You have judged everything that I have put before you by the past; but, friend, Truth is neither bound by the past nor the present nor the future. To understand Truth, you must put aside all things that you have accumulated and not cling with fear to the past however beautiful it may be. If the past seems so fruitful to you, if the past in its decay is so dear to you, if the past holds such sway over you, why are you here? You are here because you are faced with the future. To understand the future you must put aside the past and take the future to your heart and mind and cling to it desperately as a drowning man desires air. Not merely to dwell in some distant future, but to bring that future to the immediate present is the glory of man.

I tell you, friend, One greater than your books, your rites, your religions and your beliefs, is here, and if you would learn to understand the Truth you must put aside

122

the past, however comfortable, however pleasing, however delightful it may have been, and welcome the future. If you worship and cling to the past, you will be like the dead stumps of yesterday — no waters can revive their green shoots.

As you have to build greatly, you must bring that future, Truth, and life in its fulfilment, to the present. To create greatly, to create lastingly, you must understand, and so I say: Do not follow, do not obey, do not be loyal to any person except to yourself, and then you will be loyal to every passer-by.

Do not repeat after me words that you do not understand. Do not merely put on a mask of my ideas, for it will be an illusion and you will thereby deceive yourself.

I would build in your heart and mind that Truth which is of no form and hence eternal. I would change your heart and mind in the shadow of eternity. When you change and build on the love of life and its understanding, what you build will be everlasting. I do not want to concern myself with the moulding of a door, which is but an expression of life. You can always change the expression of life, but if you would build eternally in the light of the Truth, you must ever give love to life, with new ideas and understanding to nourish it. The only eternal creation is that which is without form, with life itself and not with the expressions of life. You want me to create your expressions, to lay down disciplines for you to follow; you want me, who am the Life, to deal with the mouldings of the door. Because I do not concern myself with the expressions and manifestations of life, you are not satisfied. You want me to deal with the transitory instead of with the eternal.

Friend, I want to lay the foundation of Truth in your mind and heart. That is the work of life and therefore of the eternal. You have not so far been concerned with that foundation, you have not taken to heart and pondered over that Truth; you have all the time occupied yourself with the past, with small misunderstandings, with the corruption from obedience, with petty loyalties to individuals, with the adoration of passing mediators and *gurus*. Is it not better to seek the life eternal that shall nourish you always, than to seek shelters that vary from moment to moment, inviting you to their decay and stagnation?

Friend, believe me, I am saying all this out of the fullness of my heart. Because I am in love with that life which is in everyone, I would free that life; but you do not want that, you want the passing

love, the fleeting comfort and the balm
that shall heal your momentary pain. You
desire what you perceive, but if your
perception is limited and conditioned, your
desire will be the cause of your sorrow.
But if your perception has no limitation,
if it is beyond all beliefs and traditions,
then your desire will have no limitations;
it will be life itself. You are not in love
with life: you are in love with the past,
and life is not concerned with the past.
Life, like the swift-running waters, is
always going forward and is never still
and stagnant.

Because One greater than all these is with
you, I hold it dear and precious that you
should understand in the fullness of your
heart and mind, and so create the light
which shall be your guide, which is not
the light of another, but your own. Go
away with the mirror of Truth which

126

shall reflect your life, with the love that
is detached, and with the understanding
of the Truth.

127

**Return this book on or before the last
date stamped below.**